Survival and Peace in the Nuclear Age

Survival and Peace in the Nuclear Age

Laurence W. Beilenson

REGNERY/GATEWAY, INC.
CHICAGO

CONTENTS

Preface

In the nuclear age the question that dwarfs all others is: How are we to survive as a free people? This question is too important to leave to the politicians. The American people can solve it if we make it our business and are neither optimistic nor afraid.

Rhetoric about the beauty of peace will not help. Rather we need the realism of the founding fathers about the nature of humankind. A wiser group of leaders has never blessed the birth of any nation. Though they wore no halos, and though their opinions are not Holy Writ, their ideas are always worth consulting.

One of our most precious legacies from them is *The Federalist,* a group of newspaper articles written by Alexander Hamilton, James Madison, and John Jay to advocate ratification of the Constitution by the states. While on constitutional interpretation *The Federalist* is often cited, we have sadly neglected its wisdom about affairs abroad.

The method of *The Federalist* is as admirable as its substance. The writers are caustic about "the reveries of those political doctors whose sagacity disdains the admonitions of experimental instruction." Though none of the authors was a professional historian, the pages of *The Federalist* recount and rely upon the ancient, medieval, and modern history in which the wide reading of the authors had steeped them. We can emulate with profit.

In seeking the source of a personal misfortune, a sensible beginning is to look into a mirror. When faced with national mistakes, it is fair for us to share the blame with "those damn politicians" whom we elect. Criticizing is easier than finding workable substitutes. Lyndon Johnson's favorite question was: "What would you do?" More academically, Henry Kissinger repeatedly asked: "What are the alternatives?"

In trying to answer, the patterns of history are a surer guide than conventional wisdom. If we heed the patterns, it is impossible to keep step with current opinion. Though usually a marcher who is out of step with the tune being played is uncomfortable, occasionally he is on the true beat. And, as John Stuart Mill said, "the general or prevailing opinion . . . is rarely or never the whole truth."

In following conventional wisdom we have denied West Germany nuclear weapons and have undertaken the responsibility of West German nuclear defense. Because we possess the only nuclear forces comparable to those of the USSR, it is likely to make a nuclear assault on the United States concurrently with or before any Soviet attack on western Europe. Otherwise the Soviets would risk an American first nuclear strike with the tremendous advantage the first blow confers.

Despite such danger, every president from Harry Truman on has asserted that as the leader of the free world and pursuant to its collective security, we must continue the American military presence in West Germany. At the outset we did not intend to defend West Germany forever. But if we were to stop now, we would have to make an exception to another American policy, nuclear nonproliferation — no spread of nuclear weapons.

And there's the rub. In decency we cannot say to the West Germans: "We are going home, and you must defend yourselves, but to do so you may not have any nuclear weapons." If nuclear nonproliferation is our guide star, we are left defending West Germany forever or until nuclear war breaks out. Is allowing West Germany to have nuclear weapons a greater peril than our military presence there?

This question is raised here because its treatment does not begin until Chapter 6. Chapters 2-5 — about armed might and its supposed alternatives — may seem to favor the hawks. Chapter 6 — about disposing our military forces so as to avoid war — may seem to be on the side of the doves. The common thread of all the chapters, however, is that each suggested alternative is bolstered by historical patterns and tends to contribute to our survival and to keeping the peace.

Epithets are a poor substitute for reason. Except for a few communists who try to undermine our institutions, Americans are not enemies of each other. Hawks and doves, like liberals and conservatives, both cherish the United States. Abroad all of us sail in the same ship of state. Our common interest in survival and peace is more basic than our differences.

The founders of our country were optimistic about the ability of the United States to survive as a free nation in a world where there was little freedom. With clear eyes and brave hearts we can do as well in our even more dangerous world.

✿　✿　✿　✿　✿

Because this book relies on historical patterns, its sources have to be many descriptive political and military histories of the countries of the world. My previous two books contained 143 pages of notes, references, and bibliographies. Although my research for this book has been no less thorough, I have omitted those appendages save for the footnotes, which I have endeavored to keep to a minimum.

I am grateful for the editorial help of my editor Mr. Benjamin Barrett, of my cousin Edna Beilenson, and of Dorothy Macdonald, and I thank the friends who criticized the much longer previous drafts of this book. Its faults are my own.

CHAPTER 1

To Survive as a Free People

We can dissipate the winds of oratory that envelop us by answering these fundamental questions: What is our paramount aim? In what kind of international environment do we operate? How do we break down foreign policy to its simple basics?

We chart our course according to the destination we seek to reach. Unless we know where we are trying to go, we are unlikely to get there, but nothing seems easier than ascertaining the paramount objective of the United States abroad. The propensity of politicians to complicate and embroider, however, has obscured the simple.

American statesmen have proclaimed our goals abroad in a series of high-flown slogans, such as preserving the liberty of free men everywhere and providing a peaceful world in which our children can live. In selecting our objectives we have not confined ourselves to such sentiments. In 1947 we adopted containment of communism as an American aim; in 1972 we superimposed détente on containment. Military men and their political superiors have added specific objectives: the preservation of the North Atlantic Treaty Organization (NATO), maintaining our Japanese alliance, keeping the sea lanes open to secure American access to raw materials.

The founding fathers were more modest and simple about our foreign aims, which our Constitution twice states as "the common Defence and general Welfare of the United States." The purpose of the common defense obviously is survival, but the founding fathers were not content for the American people merely to survive physically. A stated aim of the Constitution is to "secure . . . liberty to ourselves, and our Posterity." *The Federalist* is in accord. But were the Constitution and *The Federalist* silent, common sense would tell us that our paramount national objective abroad is survival as a free people.

Since the birth of our nation, we have argued about how the general welfare is to be promoted — and shared — at home. But in affairs abroad *The Federalist* leaves no room for argument that promoting the general welfare of the United States was intended to include its material prosperity.

Sometimes our actions seem to have put our prosperity ahead of our survival as a free people. The two aims are not on a par; in importance there is a vast gulf between survival as a free people and general welfare or prosperity. Though the Constitution is silent as to which is our prime aim, No. 3 of *The Federalist* states: "Among the many objects to which a wise and free people find it necessary to direct their attention, that of providing for their *safety* seems to be the first."

If *The Federalist* were silent on which of our aims abroad is paramount, again common sense would fill the void. To discuss the general welfare of a conquered people is a contradiction in terms. It is equally contradictory to talk about the welfare of the 100 million Americans dead in a nuclear war. Our survival as a free people comes first; the general welfare or national prosperity of the United States is our objective only when the action or inaction contemplated will not endanger that survival.

A free nation has the right to subordinate its material well-being to such virtues as kindness and generosity and is honored by such a choice. Neither of our goals requires us to stuff ethics into a box stored in the basement and forgotten. Nor do our objectives preclude a concern for the rest of the world. But the objectives of the Constitution are the common defense and general welfare of the United States, not of the world. As the founding fathers knew, the leaders of other nations will look after their own; the duty of the political leaders of the United States is to protect the people of the United States.

It has been said that our aims abroad are to survive and perchance to flourish. Amended slightly, this felicitous phrase expresses our attainable, unifying, and simple objectives abroad: to survive as a free people and perchance to flourish.

The founding fathers assumed that war between nations was normal, an assumption warranted by history and their own personal experience. During 50 of the 67 years of George Washington's life, war was being waged in Europe. In our own day it is still beyond the power of the United States to insure a peaceful world, but in the nuclear era, keeping the United States at nuclear peace, though subordinate to survival, keeps close company with it. While the destructiveness of nuclear weapons has been commonly overstated, they are destructive enough to command our utmost endeavor to stay at nuclear peace. The deaths of half of us might or might not mean the demise of the United States as a free nation. But preventing such slaughter is so akin to our paramount aim that it becomes part of it.

For our prime goal we have substituted policies, one of which was containment of communism. Our blunders in execution have been legion, but it was stubborn pursuit of the policy, without checking at each step how it accorded with our prime objective, that visited upon us our Vietnamese tragedy. We started our entanglement early in the administration of Harry S. Truman when we heavily subsidized the French effort to suppress the Vietnamese rebellion led by Ho Chih Minh. Since 1920 Ho had served Moscow loyally in Europe and Asia, and he had been a senior officer of the Far Eastern Section of the Comintern. In Vietnam he ably manipulated the national movement against French rule to serve his steadfast purpose to place his communist party in control of the government. Ho was devoted to violence, brutally cruel, mendacious, and deceitful; in short he was a good communist. We correctly judged that any successful movement headed by him would bring communist rule, which we assumed to be irreversible. The people's revolt against the French, however, was primarily national and ethnic. Because the French were not communists and our policy was to contain communism, we supported French colonial rule.

Dwight D. Eisenhower continued to uphold the French. When they were in dire straits, the hawks in his administration urged him to intervene militarily. We had to, they reasoned, to hold the line against communism. To his credit, Eisenhower rejected the advice. Instead he decided to hold the line in the South. After France quit and Ho ruled at Hanoi, Eisenhower bolstered Ngo Dien Diem as ruler of South Vietnam with American money, arms, and military trainers of the South Vietnamese army. In 1959 a few American soldiers were killed in battle in South Vietnam.

John F. Kennedy further committed the United States to Diem and sent more military advisers. By December 1962 our forces in Vietnam numbered 4,000. In 1963 it seemed to Kennedy that Diem's continued rule jeopardized our policy; so we connived in the coup that overthrew and killed Diem.

Without withdrawing our support, we tolerated further coups during Lyndon Johnson's administration. At his request in 1964-1965 Congressional resolutions and military appropriations brought us into an undeclared war with North Vietnam.

Each president performed his duties to his country as he saw them. Those duties, however, became encased in a dominant policy that generated its own momentum.

In his marginal annotations to Karl von Clausewitz *On War*, V. I. Lenin asked a pertinent question: "Is policy the main thing?" Conventional wisdom replies "Yes," but the correct answer is "No." The best foreign policy is not to have one; our two aims are sufficient guides. A policy interposed between our paramount objective and the situation can distort the objective, warp our estimate of the situation, and lose sight of the capacity and limitations of each tool of statecraft. This is what happened to us in Vietnam where we followed the policy of containing communism.

Our danger in specific areas is heightened by the general amorality that has marked the actions of governments abroad. While often flickering, the flame of an ideal has glowed in the founding and history of the United States. Our nation, though not always practicing righteousness, has yearned for it. But in affairs abroad of moment no great power ever has observed a high ethical standard for long. We need not conform, but we must know; for a major threat to our survival as a free people is inherent in the nature of nations.

The international world is a high-sounding phrase to describe a group of nations composed of human beings. Unlike the founding fathers who read the Good Book, some of our secular idealists look at foreign affairs through the spectacles of the world as it should be. Praiseworthy though such good intentions may be, any hope of realization must start with man as he is, as do both Judaism and Christianity. The chosen people commenced their backsliding in Genesis and continued through the last book of the Old Testament. Had it not been so, the Hebrew prophets' stirring call to repent would have been unnecessary. Christianity accepts sin as part of the human condition, to be redeemed through the saving grace of Christ. And the historical portions of the Bible portray men and their rulers as anything but benign.

In *The Federalist* (No. 51), James Madison wrote:

It may be a reflection on human nature that such devices should be necessary to control the abuses of government. But what is government itself but the greatest of all reflections on human nature? If men were angels, no government would be necessary. If angels were to govern men, neither external nor internal controls on government would be necessary.

Probably Madison had not read the memorandum to Louis XVI of France from Caron de Beaumarchais, our supplier of munitions before France entered our Revolutionary War. Beaumarchais, a noted playwright, described human nature scathingly:

Were men angels, political ways might . . . be disdained
. . . . But if men were angels, there would be no need of religion to enlighten them, of laws to govern them, of magistrates to restrain them, of soldiers to subdue them; and the earth, instead of being a faithful image of hell, would be indeed a celestial abode.[1]

As the Bible and all literature teach, man has a dual nature torn between good and evil. After recognizing benevolent impulses, the philosopher George Santayana (1863-1952) asserted that "all living creatures become wicked under pressure."[2] As our founding fathers knew, men are inherently selfish. Winston S.

1. J. Durand, *New Materials for the History of the American Revolution*, Henry Holt, New York, 1889, p. 68.
2. G. Santayana, *Dominations and Powers*, Scribner's, New York, 1951, p. 436.

Churchill observed that since history began men have not "appreciably" improved in virtue.[3]

A gloomy opinion of human nature is unnecessary to uphold the good sense of vigilance against evildoers. One may believe that most human beings are inherently good now and argue that human nature will improve, but only the willfully blind can fail to see that a large number of persons keep the police busy. Crime can be punished, but no nation has ever succeeded in abolishing it. For the foreseeable future, even though the evil ones are in the minority, they still will require us to keep up our guard.

Whether governments or statesmen have been worse than ordinary men is debatable; certainly they have been no better. Niccolò Machiavelli (1469-1527) did not originate lack of political ethics; he merely chronicled what had been standard operating procedure, while the twentieth century cynicism of Charles de Gaulle was grounded upon the history of nations. Pragmatically honesty has not always been in the national interest. Elizabeth I of England said that she liked to wage war "underhand," and Frederick the Great of Prussia delighted in his infidelity to allies, but the deceits of both sovereigns advanced the fortunes of their countries. We enjoy our own bounteous land through the fraud and violence against the Indians and others practiced by our pioneers, who, though giants in the earth, were not moral paragons.

Communist ethics, as formulated by V. I. Lenin, and as they have been practiced ever since, are simply a lack of ethics as we understand them. The aim of all Leninists is rule by a communist party of every government on earth. Whatever promotes that end — no matter how abhorrent to conventional bourgeois ethics — is good; whatever hinders that goal is bad. There is no room for misunderstanding, for Lenin was refreshingly frank. Nor have communist ethics mellowed. In his 1976 report to the 25th Congress of the Communist Party of the Soviet Union, Leonid I. Brezhnev said: "We may recall Lenin's words that in our society

3. W. S. Churchill, *The Aftermath 1918-1928*, Scribner's, New York, 1929, p. 483.

all is moral that serves the interest of building communism."[4] Such sophistry sanctifies foul deeds by assumed goods ends.

The ancient Greeks were as frank as Lenin and Brezhnev. According to H. G. Wells, the history of the Greek city states "is a story of narrow rivalries and inexplicable hatreds."[5] The Greeks, however, had a simple explanation for the wars they waged: the nature of men and of nations. Thucydides makes this apparent all through his classic history of the Peloponnesian War (431-404 B.C.).

The war was the final eruption in the long smoldering hostility between Athens and Sparta. Before the war started, delegations from the allies of Sparta gathered there for a debate on war or peace. Some Athenian representatives who were in Sparta on other business were also given the opportunity to present the case for Athens. One of the remarks by the spokesman for the Athenians epitomized their candor: "We have done nothing extraordinary, nothing contrary to human nature in accepting an empire . . . and then in refusing to give it up. . . . It has always been a rule that the weak should be subject to the strong."[6] From then on, personal and national interests have relegated ethics to the nethermost hold of the ship of state.

This is evident from the story of nations abroad. That story has been the history of the tools of statecraft, as becomes apparent by tracing the steps through which foreign policy is made.

The statesman can keep his options open, that is, postpone; thereby he has chosen to do nothing today. A nation makes its foreign policy by a series of executed decisions to do nothing or something now. Sometimes doing nothing is the wiser course.

Before deciding to do something, the statesman weighs responses; for in contrast to a carpenter sawing an inanimate board, national action brings reaction, and in a possibly widening circle. The reaction also may come from a decision to do nothing.

If the statesman elects to act, his decision necessarily requires a selection of one or more of the tools of statecraft. Before the

4. L. I. Brezhnev, 1976 report to 25th Congress of Communist Party Soviet Union, reported in *Isvestiya*, February 25, 1976.

5. H. G. Wells, *The Outline of History,* Macmillan, New York, 1927, p. 317.

6. Thucydides, *History of the Peloponnesian War,* Book 1, Ch. 6.

Peloponnesian War, Athenian expansion gradually had convinced the Spartans that their main political goal was to prevent Athenian hegemony in Greece. The discussion at Sparta immediately preceding the war reviewed the situation. King Archidamus of Sparta, after stressing the sea power and wealth of Athens, advocated diplomacy to delay:

> Meanwhile, we should be making our own preparations by winning over new allies both among Hellenes and . . . foreigners — from any quarter, in fact, where we can increase our naval and financial resources. . . . If [the Athenians do not] pay attention to our diplomatic protests, . . . then, after two or three years have passed, we shall be in a much sounder position and can attack them.[7]

Other Spartans successfully argued for immediate war. If Archidamus had prevailed, probably war would have come later. The decision to be made then and there, however, was to choose either diplomacy or war.

Every significant action abroad employs a tool of statecraft. The statesman can talk or write to another nation. That is diplomacy, the tool of communication. He can make a contract — a treaty, the instrument of agreement. He can purchase a desired action or inaction from another nation — subsidy. He can bribe an official of a foreign government to forward an enterprise of his own nation. He can disseminate words widely to influence — propaganda. He can use external subversion by aiding internal subversion in another country in order to obtain an advantage for his own nation either to influence inaction or action by the government subverted (an influencing subversion) or for the purpose of overthrowing the government (a decisive subversion). He can exert economic pressure through an embargo, cartel pricing, or similar devices either to profit his own nation financially or to coerce desired foreign action or inaction. He can arm his nation and dispose its forces to avoid war, to deter war, or to prepare for war — armed might. He can wage defensive or offensive war. Together with intelligence, the lamp for illuminating the situation, these comprise all the significant tools of statecraft.

7. Thucydides, *Peloponnesian War*, Book 1, Ch. 6.

If a nation acts abroad, it does so by using one or more of these implements, and the statesman's decision will be right only by accident unless he knows what each tool can and cannot do. Without such rudimentary knowledge a craftsman in a lesser trade soon would be out of a job. Yet throughout history, it has been a rare statesman who has thoroughly comprehended the capabilities and limitations of all the tools of his trade.

In an estimate of the situation, the salient characteristics of the tools are rarely mentioned; they are assumed to be known. But though the estimate is silent, the capacity and limits of each tool are as important as the immediate aspects of the situation. Hence, a decision to act also must answer the question: By what tool?

Because experience teaches better than logic, experience is the guide to the operation of the tools. Because history contains a longer and wider experience than the life of any person, history becomes the source from which to discover how the tools have worked and therefore how they will function.

This statement has not gone unchallenged. Some contemporary commentators tell us that history has become irrelevant because our age is unique. Most ages have fancied themselves as unique; ours is especially plagued by this conceit because of the miracles of science. But since the fruits of scientific discoveries must be administered by human beings, the uniqueness mostly disappears. Not entirely, however. In contrast with the slow pace of other ages, material progress has increased rapidly since the industrial revolution of the nineteenth century, and, following the dropping of an atom bomb on Hiroshima in 1945, with giant strides. But from the dawn of history to the present, defective human nature has not changed appreciably. The two underlying basics of our affairs abroad are: Swift further advances in weapons are to be expected; a significant alteration in the nature of men or nations is not to be expected. Though both are fair extrapolations of history, the human nature basic is more reliable because it is supported by an unchanging pattern.

If the study of history could answer all questions, the statesman's task would be easy. Alas, history provides no such magic wand; there is no open sesame to the door of judgment. Nor is history a god to worship or a substitute for virtue, religion, or philosophy. History is merely the best source of experience.

Perhaps because the founding fathers were not subjected to the babble from our many towers, they read and reflected on history. It is no accident, therefore, that *The Federalist* used historical patterns in exploring the course of affairs abroad.

Unlike the founding fathers, Karl von Clausewitz discourses on the misapplication of history, and in a more recent book on strategy General André Beaufre asserts that history can be used to prove any conclusion.[8] Each then employs historical examples throughout the book in which he deprecates them. Certainly history can be misused if examples are cited without regard to contrary examples; naturally precedents do not always fall into a neat arrangement to indicate a conclusion; and of course history does not exactly repeat itself because no two situations are precisely alike. The stress on difference, however, diverts attention from the common characteristics that unite to form the patterns which history weaves.

Professor Arthur M. Schlesinger, Jr. has written frequently and brilliantly on the inscrutability of history as a guide to the future. As he points out, the historical method often has abashed its expositors. The rule to be derived is the inherent uncertainty of particular future events. In discussing the vagaries of history, however, Schlesinger notes an exception. After quoting the historian Crane Brinton about the "nonsense" of the doctrine of the absolute uniqueness of historical events, Schlesinger agrees that generalizations about the past, "defective as they may be," are possible and can strengthen the capacity of statesmen to deal with the future.[9]

In proper emphasis Schlesinger's exception is more important than his rule. Simple generalizations about the past need not be defective as a guide for the future. Certainly the nature of nations and of their lack of ethics abroad can be ascertained from history. The effectiveness of the statesman's tools, their char-

8. Karl von Clausewitz, *On War*, Book 2, Ch. 6; Général d'Armée André Beaufre, *An Introduction to Strategy*, Frederick A. Praeger, New York, 1965, p. 14.

9. A. M. Schlesinger, Jr., *The Bitter Heritage*, Fawcett Crest, New York, 1967, p. 91.

acteristics, and the ability or inability of each tool to accomplish an objective can be discovered from the historical pattern of the functioning of each tool. For example, whether treaties will keep the peace can be found out by determining whether treaties have kept the peace.

The bulk of the literature on how foreign policy is made stresses the maneuvers within the bureaucracy. When the buck stops on the presidential desk, however, the process by which decisions are made is, as Clausewitz said about strategy, "very simple, but not on that account very easy."[10]

By whatever name, estimating the situation is an ancient and continuing manner of reaching a decision. After stating the objective, the United States army divides its assay of the situation into three parts: (1) our own strengths and weaknesses; (2) the strengths and weaknesses of the enemy; (3) surrounding circumstances. Formally or informally governments follow the same method of estimating in affairs abroad.

For gauging enemy strengths and weaknesses, military men have adopted a standard that is endlessly mooted between the Pentagon and its antimilitary critics: the doctrine of capabilities. The military theory of western schools of war and of the Soviet Union teaches that the estimate of the situation must be based on enemy capabilities rather than on enemy intentions. The commander must not try to guess what the enemy *will* do but instead must appraise what the enemy *can* do.

Though theory has placed the doctrine of capabilities firmly in the judgment seat, practice of the doctrine has not been an open sesame to success in war. In the outcome of battles, the doctrine of enemy capabilities frequently has proved inferior to guessing enemy intentions. A classic example is the justly admired Valley campaign of Major General Thomas J. Jackson. At the first battle of Bull Run he earned his nickname of Stonewall; in the Valley campaign he resembled lightning.

In March 1862 General George B. McClellan, commanding the Union Army of the Potomac, moved to attack Richmond. Against his 100,000 Union soldiers the Confederates could mus-

10. Karl von Clausewitz, *On War*, Book 3, Ch. 1.

ter only 60,000; should General Irvin McDowell's 40,000 men join forces with McClellan, Richmond seemed doomed.

Stonewall Jackson, commanding a small force in the lower Shenandoah Valley, was reinforced to a strength of almost 18,000 men and ordered to divert the largest possible Union force from McClellan. In the campaign that followed Jackson paid no attention to capabilities.

Jackson was menaced by two Union forces. Nathaniel Banks was coming from the north with 23,000 men and John C. Frémont was advancing from West Virginia with 15,000 men. Leaving 8,000 men to hold Banks, Jackson moved swiftly. First he defeated Frémont's leading elements. Then he threw a Federal garrison out of Front Royal. Then he defeated Banks at Winchester and chased him across the Potomac River. As a result, McDowell did not make his planned junction with McClellan. The Confederate purpose was achieved.

In six weeks, with fewer than 18,000 men, Jackson frustrated 70,000 Union troops and changed the whole Federal plan of campaign. Had he acted on what the superior Union forces were capable of doing to him, there would have been no Valley campaign.

When commanders have disregarded enemy capabilities and won battles, they have been praised as daring. When commanders have disregarded enemy capabilities and been defeated, they have been criticized as rash. The history of war has woven no pattern to indicate a rule.

If the doctrine of capabilities, a military theory, is an uncertain gauge during war, should it nonetheless be employed as our standard of judgment during peace?

The time line between peace and war is an instant. At one moment a nation is at peace; at the next it is under attack. It has been ever thus. The 1672 Anglo-French war against Holland began when the English navy opened fire on the Dutch merchant fleet in the English Channel; a declaration of war had been deliberately delayed to insure surprise. We complained bitterly about the perfidy of the assault on Pearl Harbor, but Japan had begun all its modern wars with surprise attacks. The USSR did not burden itself with declaring war before assailing Finland in 1939 or invading Czechoslovakia in 1968. Today we live under the shadow of the volcano. Its eruption may be sudden.

Estimating enemy capabilities has not been an open door to victory in war. Yet such estimates are a sensible standard in guarding against surprise attack when we are at peace. Two examples illustrate the reason.

When Germany attacked the USSR in 1941, the facts do not admit of any doubt that Adolf Hitler achieved surprise, and not only because the Soviet forces were not on the alert. Joseph Stalin believed in the defense in depth by which in 1814 Russia had repelled Napoleon's invasion. Nonetheless, at the time of the Nazi attack Stalin had stationed nearly 170 divisions — five-sevenths of the USSR's total number — in forward positions. This helped Hitler's capture of huge numbers of Soviet soldiers during his first drive. While the Soviet Union escaped subjugation in spite of the surprise, the damage would have been far less extensive if before the attack Stalin had said to himself: "Though I don't think Hitler will attack me, he can. So I'll pull back the bulk of my forces and keep my army and air force alerted."

Inconceivably, less than six months after Germany surprised the USSR, Japan surprised the United States. The historian Samuel Eliot Morison correctly ascribed our defeat at Pearl Harbor to our failure to observe the doctrine of capabilities:

> Although often warned against this manner of thinking, military men are apt to base action upon what they think the enemy will probably do, rather than explore and make a correct estimate of everything he can do. . . . That is exactly what happened here.[11]

All the reasons for our surprise would have been obviated if we had clung to the standard of capabilities.

The reason for a rule is the key to its application, limit, or extension. Capabilities are an uncertain gauge during war, when prudence should be balanced by daring. Conversely, capabilities are the proper measuring rod for guarding against surprise attack during peace, when nothing is to be gained by daring, and prudence is indicated. During peace, not enemy intentions but enemy capabilities are the appropriate standard for estimating

11. S. E. Morison, *History of United States Naval Operations in World War II*, v. 3, Little, Brown, Boston, 1950, p. 131.

enemy armed might because during peace, not daring but prudence is the canon for our safety. Moreover, enemy intentions are subjective and hard to ascertain, and an enemy can quickly change its mind.

By peeling off the complexities of capabilities, the simplicity of applying prudence emerges. If to our paramount objective we add prudence, if we recognize the nature of nations, if we learn from the historical operation of each tool of statecraft what it can and cannot accomplish, we can survive as a free people in this dangerous world.

CHAPTER 2

Is Nuclear War Likely?

Whatever may be true in the kingdom of heaven, nothing except individual death is inevitable on this earth. Whether nuclear war is inevitable is therefore the wrong question. The right question is whether nuclear war is to be reasonably expected sooner or later.

Though the founding fathers could not address that inquiry, their attitude offers a clue to the answer. *The Federalist* urged the necessity of union because sooner or later America would be at war. This reason was not disputed even by Thomas Jefferson, the most pacific of the founding fathers. To George Washington, who had fought in two wars, the notion of a United States perpetually at peace was unthinkable. And because the founding fathers were realistically pessimistic about the nature of nations, they would have entertained no doubt that in a major war any government would use any weapon it possessed, no matter how destructive.

Ever since scientists invented the atom bomb, some of them have been enthusiastic about banning it. The preambles of numerous United Nations resolutions express the same hope. Apart from the unreliability of treaties designed to ban weapons, realization is precluded by the many thousands of human heads in which nuclear knowledge is lodged. Even if all nuclear weapons were destroyed, phoenix-like they would rise again. Some nation would suspect that another nation had secretly kept old nuclear weapons or was manufacturing new ones and would hasten to do likewise. Unless displaced by arms at least as lethal, nuclear weapons are here to stay.

15

Even hawks do not dare to predict nuclear war. Instead they speak of nuclear blackmail, which may be defined: If in the 1962 Cuban missile crisis we threatened the USSR with nuclear war, that was self-defense; if to gain political advantage the USSR should threaten us with nuclear war, that would be nuclear blackmail. Threats by either side can bring nuclear war. In 1962 Nikita Khrushchev backed down in the Cuban missile confrontation; someday a leader on one side or the other may not.

The twentieth century prophets of peace have unwittingly appropriated a phrase used in *The Communist Manifesto* by the nineteenth century prophets of violence Karl Marx and Friedrich Engels, the "interdependence of nations." In 1910, only four years before World War I, Norman Angell published *The Great Illusion*, which proved that in his enlightened era war between the great powers should be impossible because of their economic interdependence. War had become unprofitable; so no government should be foolish enough to start one. Viscount Reginald Esher, the trusted adviser of the King of England, felt sure that Germany was as receptive to Angell's cogent analysis as Britain. Translated into 11 languages, *The Great Illusion* became prevailing British opinion, especially at the universities and among the elite.

World War I came and went, time passed, and optimism revived. In 1929 Winston S. Churchill said that the 1922 Treaty of Washington among Japan, Britain, the United States, and other nations regulated and insured the peace of the Pacific. Churchill was equally impressed by the 1925 Locarno pacts to keep the peace among Germany, Belgium, France, Britain, Italy, Poland, and Czechoslovakia.[1] About the new "spirit of Locarno" the French statesman Aristide Briand expressed the general opinion on both sides of the Atlantic: "We have done with the long period of terrible and sanguinary conflicts which have stained the pages of history."[2]

1. W. S. Churchill, *The Aftermath 1918-1928*, Scribner's, New York, 1929, pp. 485-489.

2. A. Briand, quoted in F. L. Benns, *Europe Since 1914*, Crofts, New York, 1930, p. 343.

World War II came and went, time passed, and optimism revived again. Contrast the founding fathers. To them the blood with which the pages of history had been stained conveyed a message of simple import: repetition. Despite the endless argument about the reasons for wars, there can be no argument about the simplest and best known historical pattern — the constant recurrence of war through the ages. This pattern will not tell us when or where the next war will break out, but it will tell us that the outbreak of war is likely.

Is nuclear war different because of the great damage it will inflict? Hand to hand combat is as brutal as bombing, and a man killed by a spear is as dead as a man killed by a nuclear missile. In ancient wars sometimes all the men of the defeated tribe or nation were killed and the women and children taken into captivity. In reciting the iniquities of George III, our Declaration of Independence proclaimed:

He . . . has endeavoured to bring on the inhabitants of our frontiers, the merciless Indian savages, whose known rule of warfare, is an undistinguished destruction of all ages, sexes and conditions.

The Thirty Years' War (1618-1648) devastated and decimated Germany. Civilized Rome utterly destroyed Carthage. Nor during World War II did the British and Americans shrink from mass destruction in fire raids on Hamburg, Dresden, and Tokyo or in bombing civilians. In the 1970s the Cambodians experienced the horror of conquest by infantry. And in 1945 the United States dropped the atom bomb.

Still, since most differences are of degree, is not the vast destruction that will be wrought by nuclear war a distinction? Not when another pattern of history is pondered: Man has used every weapon he has ever devised. Until and including atomic weapons, there has been not a single exception to the rule. Put this pattern together with the pattern of recurrence of war, and unless nuclear weapons are superseded by more lethal inventions, it takes no crystal ball to perceive that a nuclear war is likely sooner or later.

The patterns have been no accident; they are inherent in the nature of man. True, among the great majority of humankind, the good outweighs the bad, and kindness overbalances cruelty. But there have been, and, until the good Lord sees fit to change human nature, there always will be criminals. Of this ilk the worst in violence — as in thievery — have been the rulers on this earth.

In history's chamber of horrors, rulers occupy most of the niches. Sultan Mohammed III (1593-1603), who killed all of his 19 brothers, was matched in the west by the headsman's ax and the guillotine. If Uganda's Idi Amin is ranked as a monster of the 1970s, he merely takes his place beside Russia's Ivan The Terrible (1530-1584) and Peter the Great (1672-1725). Consider the ideologues of the twentieth century. V. I. Lenin murdered the Russian royal family and wiped out a large part of his nation's bourgoisie in the sacred name of communism. As Count Wilhelm von Mirbach, the German foreign minister at Petrograd, wrote in a 1918 dispatch: "The government is following the well-tried formula: If you won't be my brother I'll beat your brains in. . . ."[3] For the good of mankind, Joseph Stalin and Mao Tse-tung (Zedong) killed millions of their countrymen. These dictators flew the flag of ideology, a banner oft drenched in blood. Finally, one name is enough: Hitler.

If all the human beings murdered since Cain killed Abel could be called forth from their shrouds, their number would be tiny compared to the countless millions slain in war because of the greed, ambition, and thirst for glory of the rulers on this earth. And to start a nuclear war it takes only one such ruler.

Our optimists would characterize such an analysis as a worst case projection to meet a mythical peril. After all, they say, we do not face numerous adversaries with formidable nuclear weapons; we face only the Soviet Union. Against it Americans can be confident about their safety; the Russians are not coming, and neither is nuclear war. Our political guardians have adopted a plan to fit the realistic facts. We are insured against nuclear war because we deter it by our official policy of mutual assured destruction.

Critics of mutual assured destruction call it by its acronym: MAD. This is unfair to the presidents, secretaries of defense, and

3. Z. A.B. Zeman, ed., *Germany and the Revolution in Russia 1915-1918, Documents from the Archives of the German Foreign Ministry*, Oxford University Press, London, 1958, p. 117.

joint chiefs of staff who have accepted the doctrine to which Congress has assented. Mutual assured destruction has a logical and rational basis, which deserves a fair statement. The theory holds that defense against nuclear weapons is impossible. The USSR and the United States each has such a tremendous number of nuclear warheads that either country can inflict such horrendous loss of life and property on the other as to be unacceptable to either. Accordingly, the only escape of both adversaries from that calamity is to assure mutual destruction of both if nuclear war occurs, thereby assuring that nuclear war will not occur. By removing all defense a stable balance is assured. That having been demonstrated, nuclear war will not happen. As a corollary, anything which disturbs the balance of destruction is "destablizing," "provocative," and must be eschewed like a plague.

The theory has some strange twists of simple thinking. Its proponents contend that preparing to defend ourselves is a mistake. Even more curious is their assumption that defense is provocative, but pointing a loaded gun at the heart of our opponent is not.

The doctrine is mutual only in name. As Secretary of Defense Harold Brown's annual report to Congress for fiscal year 1981 concedes, the Soviets reject the theory. The abundant Soviet literature on nuclear war holds that nuclear war still is war in which attack and defense interact, and that defense is as important as attack.

Nor is Soviet destruction assured. The official teaching of the Soviet Union maintains that with the civil defense the USSR has created, the casualties of the Soviets in a nuclear war will not exceed their casualties in World War II. For the purpose of deterring nuclear war, it is immaterial whether the calculation is correct. Deterrence is psychological; for it to work the opponent must believe as we do. As Secretary of Defense Harold Brown put it in 1978: "What would deter us might not deter them."

George F. Kennan tells us that the Soviet rulers are old, and old men do not start wars. When Emperor Franz Josef of Austria attacked Serbia to start World War I, he was close to his eighty-fourth birthday. Kennan further assures us that the present rulers of the USSR want peace.[4] As these lines are written, Leonid Brezhnev is in ill health. But on whether nuclear war is to be reasonably expected sooner or later, there is no need to dwell on what the current Soviet leaders think. As Genesis recounts, after Jacob's son Joseph became powerful in Egypt, the people of Israel followed him, multiplied, and grew prosperous. Chapter 1 of Exodus relates why their persecution began: "Now there arose up a new king over Egypt, which knew not Joseph." The management changed and with it the attitude of the ruler.

Without being displaced, rulers often have changed their minds, to which tendency should be added a swift emotional shift. Russian reporters have stated that in his last weeks Stalin was paranoid; American reporters have claimed that in his final days in the White House Richard Nixon was sometimes drunk and in a state of mind bordering on the psychotic. Believing either report is unnecessary; it is enough to realize that many rulers have been drunkards, psychotics, or just plain fools. In our day one of these types may control the nuclear button on either side.

The fatal flaw in mutual assured destruction is the doctrine's reliance on logical and rational behavior, epitomized in a 1978 statement to Congress by Secretary of Defense Brown: "We do not propose to plan against total irrationality."[5] As the founding fathers reiterated, logic and reason have not been the only propellants of the ship of state; its sails have billowed before the winds of emotion. Frequently the helmsman has turned the tiller according to his passion, including anger, pride, and lust for dominance. True, self-interest and prudence often have prevailed; equally true, often they have not. Only the unreasonable believe that rulers always act reasonably. If rulers had acted rationally, the pages of history would not reek with the smell of blood. And to start a nuclear war it takes only one spell of emotion or passion by one ruler of the USSR or of the United States.

When Fred C. Iklé was Director of our Arms Control and Disarmament Agency, his 1974 speech to the Harvard-MIT Arms

4. G. F. Kennan, *The Cloud of Danger*, Little, Brown, Boston, 1977, p. 180 and passim.

5. H. Brown, *Annual Defense Department Report FY1979*, p. 5.

Control Seminar gave other reasons why mutual deterrence does not guarantee prevention of nuclear war:

Because nuclear strategy cannot offer positive proof, . . . it is more like a theology than a science. . . . Many of you are familiar with calculations of so-called "missile exchanges" — often referred to in arms control literature and in congressional debates. These calculations continue to be prominent in our thinking because we really know how to do them. Much as in a freshman's algebra test, we have tailored the problem to our capability to calculate. The seemingly rigorous models of nuclear deterrence are built on the rule, "What you can't calculate you leave out." . . .

Our entire structure of thinking about deterrence lacks empiricism. . . . There can be no trial and error here, no real learning. . . . The more battle experience military analysts have, the more modest they become in predicting the course of conventional war. But about nuclear war, we pretend that we can analyze all that is relevant. . . .

How can we know what factors to credit for the fact that nuclear weapons have not been used since August 1945? The formidable confrontation of massive and complicated missile forces that we face today has lasted for one decade only. . . .

The danger of relying on naked deterrence is heightened by the current emphasis on speed in planning the response to a nuclear attack. . . . The unpredictable perils of split-second alert and launching procedures could create a situation in which there is absolutely no time for correction. . . .

Our efforts to prevent nuclear war could fail . . . not only because of an inadequate retaliatory capability to deter a deliberate attack, but for other reasons, such as an accident, an unintended process of escalation, or a combination of failures and causes we could not have anticipated or even imagined. Put in such terms, no one ever disagrees with the proposition that a situation of mutual deterrence does not by itself guarantee the prevention of nuclear war. Yet nearly everyone keeps debating arms control policies and nuclear strategy in terms of naked deterrence.[6]

Another reason an American-Soviet nuclear war may occur in spite of deterrence is a Soviet scientific breakthrough that would nullify or substantially blunt the effectiveness of an American second strike. This is no idle speculation. George H. Heilmeier, Director of the Pentagon's advanced research projects, said in 1977:

> Unlike any time within the past decade, there are technological initiatives on the horizon that could dramatically influence national security. Difficult technical problems remain, but these initiatives just might make our test of areas of potential technological surprise more than science fiction.

After identifying numerous areas of potential surprise Heilmeier added:

> Unfortunately, we have no monopoly on advanced technology. Soviet efforts are characterized by a massive commitment of resources — people, facilities, and capital — and it is not clear that we can get there ahead of them. Make no mistake about it — it is essential that we get there first . . .[7]

Besides the hidden research contest, the probability of a scientific breakthrough — by which side nobody can be sure — is suggested by other patterns. While until about 1860 the most striking characteristic in the history of weapons was the slow pace of change, in the next 85 years the slow walk quickened to such a fast gallop that the weapons changes from 1860 to 1945 were greater than the alterations during all preceding history. With Hiroshima and post-Hiroshima experience added, the pattern fairly shouts its message. The atom bomb delivered by long-range airplanes brought the whole of far distant populations

6. F. C. Iklé, speech February 20, 1974, Department of State *Bulletin*, March 25, 1974, v. 70, No. 1813, p. 314.

7. G. H. Heilmeier, "Technological Surprise," *National Defense*, May-June 1977, v. 61, No. 342, pp. 471, 473.

under fire for the first time. In two decades came the hydrogen bomb, intercontinental ballistic missiles, and the beginning of the penetration of outer space. From 1945 on the rapid qualitative transformation in weapons conforms to no previous experience.

To conclude that weapons will resume their sluggard crawl would not be a fair extrapolation of the whole pattern, but it would be a possible one were it not for a related pattern in the history of weapons that emphasizes the applicability of the major pattern: Important changes in weapons have been a concomitant of important changes in science and technology. The age of metals brought corresponding alterations in weapons. The art of weapons declined in the Dark Ages, as did learning; the age of gunpowder began during the renaissance in knowledge. Though in the early stages of the industrial revolution changes in weapons were not great, the reverse was true during the 85 years preceding Hiroshima, as science and learning expanded. Conventional weapons are pygmies to the nuclear giant just as science before Albert Einstein is a dwarf in the age of space. The large number of scientists now working and the vast improvement in their instruments of discovery argue for the future swift progress of science and with it the likelihood of rapid change in weaponry.

Another pattern further underpins the major one. It takes engineering and manufacturing to transform scientific discoveries into usable weapons. Not until the second half of the nineteenth century did the big leap in weapons begin. Correspondingly, not until the nineteenth century did engineering and manufacturing begin to catch up with the scientific renaissance of the two preceding centuries. Today, technology is advancing with the same speed as science.

If the history of weapons had been reviewed in 1850, a different conclusion would have emerged. If the history of nations had been reviewed in 1850, the same conclusion would have been as evident then as now. No pattern of material progress can be as reliable as a pattern based on human nature. Still, the history of weapons reinforces the nature of nations to compel the estimate that despite our policy — whether called deterrence or mutual assured destruction — nuclear war is reasonably to be expected sooner or later.

A persuasive argument for the success of our nuclear deterrent rests on an important difference between the nuclear age and all the ages that have gone before: In every preceding era, whatever may have been the expected fate of the vanquished, the people of the victor nation did not face the prospect of being wiped out by war. With this in mind and echoing Norman Angell, the advocates of naked deterrence claim that in a nuclear war there will be no victor because the people of the victor country plus their cities and industry will be almost totally destroyed. Hence, the unacceptable damage that our nuclear arms would inflict on the USSR by a second strike is sufficient to insure us against a Soviet first strike.

One answer to unacceptable damage by a second strike is that the Soviet Union does not concur. A more basic answer is found in the types of rulers who have started wars. It is a coincidence rather than an argument against mutual assured destruction that its acronym is MAD. It is a fact, however, that proponents of the doctrine assert that because of mutual assured destruction only a madman would resort to nuclear war. In his celebrated 1955 balance of terror speech expounding on mutual deterrence, Winston Churchill made what he called a formidable admission: "The deterrent does not cover the case of lunatics or dictators in the mood of Hitler when he found himself in his final dugout. This is a blank." The blank is large indeed; mad rulers have been common throughout history. Emperor Caligula (Gaius Caesar) of Rome, Tsar Paul of Russia, King George III of England, and King Frederick William IV of Prussia are only the beginning of a long list. And when rulers emotionally unstable or in their dotage are added, the list greatly lengthens.

Add to the rulers likely to start a nuclear war the gamblers such as Napoleon III of France and Kaiser William II. A war gamble cost each his throne. When considering gambling, recollect the rhetoric of brinkmanship of John Foster Dulles, Secretary of State in Dwight D. Eisenhower's administration. Under John F. Kennedy we were willing to hazard nuclear war rather than live under the risk of missiles in Cuba. Under Gerald Ford, Henry Kissinger refused to rule out American use of "nuclear means" in regional situations akin to Angola.[8] And ever since we have had nuclear weapons, every president has said that if the Soviets attack our European allies by conventional arms and the allied conventional weapons fail to stop the Soviets, we will make first use of nuclear arms.

The statesman who starts a nuclear war despite the risk of unacceptable damage need be neither a madman, nor emotionally unstable, nor a gambler. He may be a utopian or an ideologue who believes that the death of many millions is not too high a price to pay for the triumph of his ideal. Remember Maximilian Robespierre and his killing when he was in power during the French Revolution. Mao was furious about Nikita Khrushchev's caution in refusing to back the adventures abroad that Mao wanted to risk. Suppose Mao had commanded the Soviet Union's nuclear weapons. He has been reported to have said that he was not afraid of nuclear war because China could lose 300,000,000 people and still be strong and populous.

The Soviet ruler who starts a nuclear war may calculate that his country will not suffer unacceptable damage. Apart from civil defense, he may count on American demoralization and surrender.

About the time period, somebody is bound to quote John Maynard Keynes: "Sooner or later we are all dead." But the nation is not, and the preamble of our Constitution takes the preferably long view. In fact, our deterrence of nuclear attack has succeeded for only a short period. The USSR did not acquire atomic weapons until 1949 and has had enough nuclear weapons with which to threaten us for only a few years.

Precise predictions are fanciful; over ten years ago C.P. Snow declared that nuclear war within ten years was a statistical fact. Without attempting any such certitude, Professors Paul Doty, Richard Garwin, George Kistiakowsky, and George Rathjens, all faculty members of the Harvard-MIT Arms Control Seminar and all believers in their subjects, nevertheless agree that nuclear war by 1999 is likely.[9] But why pick a date? 1989? 1999? 2009? No

8. H. A. Kissinger, interview, *U. S. News & World Report,* March 15, 1976, v. 80, No. 11, p. 28.

9. P. Doty, R. Garwin, G. Kistiakowsky, G. Rathjens, "Nuclear War by 1999?" *Harvard,* November 1975, v. 78, No. 3, p. 19.

one knows when a nuclear war will occur. The date may be far in the future, but it is just as probable that nuclear war will start tomorrow.

The rift between the USSR and China, as long as it lasts, is a favorable factor for American nuclear peace. But the schism does not demonstrate, as the heralds of peace claim, that nuclear war is a bugbear. The split is a fact; its duration a question. In the War of the Austrian Succession (1740-1748) England was the ally of Austria; France of Prussia. The alliances were still in force in 1756 when they were reversed for the Seven Years' War (1756-1763). Britain became the ally of Prussia; France became the ally of Austria despite a rivalry of over two centuries between the Austrian Habsburg emperors and the kings of France. Frequently yesteryear's enemies have become this year's allies.

It is beyond human ken to set a date for the termination of the Sino-Soviet schism, but that it can end suddenly and soon is as true as its present existence. The 1939 Hitler-Stalin Pact came like a bolt from the blue. To be sure, the rapprochement did not last, but it lasted long enough for Hitler to dominate western Europe until the United States entered the war. The Hitlerian and communist ideologies clashed; the Soviet and Chinese ideologies join in their objective to make the world communist-governed; their difference is about the tactics to bring it about. The tactical dispute can be reconciled. No one knows whether it will be, but reaching agreement on tactics is as probable as not reaching agreement.

The split may also be rooted in personal ambition; on each side the rulers aspire to be the bosses of the communist world. A settlement of such differences is not improbable. Until the ego and power of Mao grew great, he accepted Soviet hegemony in the communist world. The Soviet leaders know they cannot hope to attain complete dominance again. Reconciliation is as probable as no reconciliation.

Some experts maintain that the Sino-Soviet dispute will not be settled without war because the national territorial claims are irreconcilable. For the greater part of the nineteenth century Britain and France had territorial disputes in Africa, which on occasion threatened war between them. The same was true between Britain and Russia in Asia. Both sets of territorial claims were settled early in this century; fear of Germany united all three countries. A common ideology may have the same result between Russia and China. Their rulers may unite in saying: We must pull together again to accomplish our mutual aim.

Some realists say that China needs more territory in the north for its immense population, and the USSR will not yield the land because the numerous Chinese scare the Russians; therefore the schism will not be mended. That is a possible guess, but China could be compensated by the USSR's allowing Chinese expansion to the south, perhaps in Burma, perhaps elsewhere. The 1904 English-French and the 1907 English-Russian cold-blooded settlements of their territorial disputes were made at the expense of weak countries in Africa and Asia. France yielded dominance to England in Egypt; England gave France a free hand in Morocco. Concurrently France and Spain divided their spheres in North Africa with British approval. Across Persia, Russia and Britain drew a geographical line. North of the line Russia was to be supreme; south of the line Britain. The settlements were monuments to the cynicism of governments.

The optimists hail the split as dissipating the myth of monolithic world communism. World communism never was as monolithic as claimed. Long before 1917 leaders both in Russia and in exile began to quarrel. Lenin himself was a splitter, but despite his and later splits, the communist movement has advanced steadily. Emphasis on the break in the monolith obscures. Even during the schism, nuclear war is not improbable for a simple reason: To wage nuclear war against the United States the USSR does not need a friendly China.

The best augury for nuclear peace is that Lenin, the mentor of the communist-ruled states, regarded subversion rather than war as the chief tool to win the world for communism. Many passages can be quoted to prove that Lenin regarded war as the chief tool. He thought that pacifists were idiots; disarmament absurd. Any war that advanced communism was holy and should be waged. According to Lenin — and he was historically correct — peace had been only a respite between wars, and in this respect history would repeat itself. In March 1919 he said:

The existence of the Soviet Republic side by side with imperialist states for a long time is unthinkable. One or the other must triumph in the end. And before that end supervenes, a series of frightful collisions between the Soviet Republic and the bourgeois states will be inevitable.

In November 1920, he declared:

We have just passed from war to peace, but . . . we have not forgotten that war will again return. As long as capitalism and socialism exist, we cannot live in peace: in the end, one or the other will triumph — a funeral dirge will be sung either over the Soviet Republic or over world capitalism.[10]

Though Lenin considered offensive war to advance communism as "holy," about the when of offensive war he was exceedingly cautious. And for a good reason. Lenin knew that most internal revolutions have needed help from a strong external national base. He was aware that the wave of rebellions that had swept Europe in 1848 had withered and died for lack of such external aid, and that the same was true of the Paris Commune revolt in 1871. He had won his Russian base for world subversion and revolution; he did not intend to risk it.

In his January 1918 argument for a separate peace with Germany, Lenin struck a significant note:

The situation in which the Socialist Revolution in Russia finds itself is to be taken as the point of departure for every definition of the international task confronting the new Soviet Government, . . . It would be very bad policy to risk the fate of the Socialist Revolution on the chance that a revolution might break out in Germany by a certain date. Such a policy would be adventurous. We have no right to take such chances.[11]

His deeds conformed. Lenin made a disadvantageous separate

10. V. I. Lenin, *Selected Works*, International Publishers, New York, 1943, v. 8, pp. 33, 296-297.

11. J. Bunyan and H. H. Fisher, *The Bolshevik Revolution, Documents and Manuscripts 1917-1918*, Stanford University Press, 1934, pp. 500-505.

peace with Germany in order not to hazard his subversive base. Not a single act during Lenin's short reign deviated from his cautious principle against adventurism in war. And in all of Lenin's published works there is not a single statement that the Soviet Union should wage offensive war where such a war would involve more than a minimal risk of losing the Soviet base for world revolution.

So far Lenin's Soviet heirs have followed his cautious attitude. Stalin settled the border clashes with Japan of the 1930s; save for them, the USSR was at peace until Hitler invaded in World War II. During it, Stalin made his 1939 safe assaults on already crippled Poland and on small Finland because he was sheltered while Germany was fighting France and England. Khrushchev's 1956 Soviet war against Hungary seemed safe with the west divided by the Anglo-French invasion of Egypt. The 1968 Brezhnev invasion of Czechoslovakia came while the United States was bogged down in Vietnam, and in each instance the USSR could have pulled back had we threatened war. Khrushchev did pull back in the 1962 Cuban missile crisis.

As new communist-ruled bases are captured, they forward the subversive master plan. But it is consistent with holding the subversive main base for subsidiary communist-ruled states to wage adventurous war, as has been done by North Korea and by Cuba in the invasion of Angola. The communists may win, and if the subsidiary base is lost, triumph in the long-range contest is not thereby irretrievably endangered.

It is possible to dispute the restraint of the Soviet leaders to date, and many analysts have. They cite the various crises which have been precipitated by the USSR since 1947, and they do not regard the foregoing Soviet actions as cautious. For example, Professor Martin Bailey, after citing a Chinese risky action, writes:

> The Soviets knowingly took an even bolder risk when they placed nuclear missiles in Cuba, . . . Thus the history of wars and crises involving U. S., Soviet, and Chinese forces through twenty-five years of nuclear deterrence is scarcely reassuring.[12]

12. M. J. Bailey, "Deterrence, Assured Destruction and Defense," *Orbis,* Fall 1972, v. 16, No. 3, pp. 684-685.

Stalin continued Lenin's caution. Subsequent rulers have become somewhat bolder. Khrushchev invaded Hungary and placed missiles in Cuba. Brezhnev could not be certain how the United States would react to the invasion of Czechoslovakia. His African forays with Cuban proxies in the 1970s have been considered adventurous by many commentators. But to know that we cannot prudently rely on Leninist caution by Soviet rulers, it is unnecessary to dispute any Soviet abstention from adventurism; Chinese lack of restraint is enough. The fact that Mao was Chinese makes no difference; he revered Lenin but took chances. To Mao, the base to be preserved with minimal risk was China. Yet his conquest of Tibet and his bombardment of Quemoy and Matsu involved more than minimal hazards that the United States might react. His 1962 invasion of India, though he later pulled back, was not Leninist caution at the time he invaded. And when he entered the Korean war he took a great risk that the United States might resort to atomic weapons.

The events of late 1978 and early 1979 should dispel any lingering doubt that communist adventurism still flourishes in spite of Lenin's admonition. Without benefit of hindsight consider Vietnam's invasion of Cambodia in late 1978. Before the incursion, China had made it plain that the consequence might be a Chinese attack on Vietnam. Even if fear of the USSR had kept the Chinese quiescent, it was nevertheless rash for Vietnam to antagonize the colossus on its northern border. To avert the peril the Vietnamese cannot count on continued Sino-Soviet animosity. Strong nations frequently have settled their disputes at the expense of weaker countries. Austria, Prussia, and Russia, though enemies, united three times to partition hapless Poland (1772, 1795, 1795-1796).

Even more reckless was the 1979 Chinese invasion of Vietnam "to teach it a lesson," when China was vulnerable to a conventional or nuclear Soviet attack. Rancorous Sino-Soviet enmity had been long and intense. The USSR had heralded its alliance with Vietnam. All China had to gain by the invasion was saving face. For that its leaders risked the survival perhaps of millions of Chinese, and certainly of the Chinese government.

Only the Soviets exhibited prudence, which they belied, however, when they invaded Afghanistan in late December, 1979. And as Afghanistan indicates, Soviet leaders may become even more adventurous.

In weighing whether nuclear war is to be reasonably expected, we should think in terms of later as well as sooner. Aside from a proper regard for our posterity, there are practical reasons. From conception to deployment in quantity nuclear weapons take about 15 years. Some of the hidden projected weapons still on the drawing boards have been there for many years. And every measure vital to our survival will take a long time to finish after we begin.

For a long-range appraisal our lens must widen beyond the USSR because the number of nations possessing nuclear weapons probably will grow. The United States, the USSR, Britain, France, and China, now have nuclear arms, India and Israel either have them or can make them, and a number of other nations have the necessary knowledge and capacity.

The history of conventional weapons predicts nuclear spread. New conventional weapons and their adaptations have spread across borders, and in modern history the spread has been rather rapid.

We have been promoting the spread of nuclear weapons. Since the "atoms for peace" program of Eisenhower, we have spent hundreds of millions of dollars on spreading nuclear technology abroad, exclusive of assistance to our allies. The 1968 Nuclear Nonproliferation Treaty institutionalized our previous practice. Art. IV provides:

All the Parties to the Treaty undertake to facilitate, and have the right to participate in, the fullest possible exchange of equipment, materials and scientific and technical information for the peaceful use of nuclear energy.

In probable violation of the treaty, since 1977 we have tried to close the barn door after the horse has left. But nations without our abundant raw materials are determined to exploit nuclear energy, our attempt is likely to fail, and peaceful uses can be transformed to weapons.

We have been insufferably self-righteous. When China and France decided to go nuclear, and when they refused to sign the nonproliferation treaty, on each occasion American and English opinion decried such callous actions as increasing the risk of nuclear war. The attitude of the five main possessing nations is utterly unreasonable. In effect they say: We five which early acquired nuclear weapons should be rewarded for our astuteness by remaining the only countries to have such arms, and in the interest of world nuclear peace other countries must refrain from acquisition and trust us to protect them. And who are the guardians of nuclear peace? The United States, which dropped the atomic bomb; the USSR, whose patron saints Marx and Lenin held that violence was the only means to bring paradise on earth; Britain and France, with their long history of wars; and China, whose mentor Mao held that power comes out of the barrel of a gun.

Under the 1968 Nuclear Nonproliferation Treaty, nations that do not possess nuclear weapons agree not to acquire them. The USSR, Britain, and the United States as possessors agree not to help others become possessors but promise to help the non-possessing signatories acquire nuclear technology for peaceful purposes. Reading the treaty, our instrument to prevent spread, suffices to show that it will not. Forget that China and France, possessing nations, have refused to sign the pact; that other nations have either not signed or not ratified it; and that treaties have been regularly broken. Forget that no inspection system is reliable; that the one under the treaty is not particularly efficient; that bribery is prevalent all over the world; and that inspectors of every kind always have been major recipients of bribes. Just remember that by express provision of the treaty every party to it can terminate its obligations under it by a notice of three months. The treaty at best is much ado about nothing; at worst it is a pact to help spread the possession of nuclear arms. Yet to obtain signatures and ratifications we have twisted many arms and paid much in concessions and foreign aid money.

Consider proliferation through the eyes of nations menaced by powerful neighbors. Can anyone seriously doubt that if Israel has not acquired nuclear weapons, with its survival at stake it will? Pakistan has lost its wars with India, which it cannot match in numbers or in conventional arms, but nuclear arms would be an equalizer. The examples can be multiplied around the world.

Suppose that each possessor gave an unambiguous promise to wage nuclear war against any attacker immediately following any such attack. With the treaty breaking record of each of the possessors, why should any nation believe it is protected by such a pledge as a deterrent? But the possessing nations have given no binding agreement to protect nonpossessing parties. And even if they had, on notice of three months any or all of the three could say: Sorry, that's all.

The main reason nuclear weapons have not spread is their cost. The cruise missile is comparatively inexpensive. Opinions differ about its effectiveness, but as a symbol it is impressive. Nuclear weapons or their successors may become simple and less expensive. When they do, they will spread widely. Even before that time, their spread to some present nonpossessors is likely. Nuclear knowledge cannot be contained; in the long run neither can nuclear weapons.

Whether our appraisal of the likelihood of nuclear war sooner or later is broad or narrows to a Soviet-American nuclear war, we would be deceiving ourselves to consider each reason in isolation; they should be totaled. Among all the reasons, however, one is chief. Engineers express the stubbornness of inanimate objects by Murphy's law: If anything can go wrong, it will. The Murphy's law of the statesman has been the recurrence of war.

Some commentators deplore such reasoning because, they say, the prediction may be self-fulfilling. In effect, they argue that in the face of danger we should, like the ostrich, bury our head in the sand. It is consistent with believing nuclear war to be probable sooner or later to do our utmost to prevent it; for neither its occurrence nor our participation is inevitable. But when we realize that despite our best efforts, nuclear war may nonetheless happen, then our preparation for survival will include preparation for our survival in spite of nuclear war. And what greater duty can an American statesman have than to provide for his nation's survival?

CHAPTER 3

Shelter and Shield

In a game of Russian roulette the player loads a revolver's cylinder with only one cartridge that can kill; the others are blanks. With his eyes turned away, he spins the cylinder and at random injects one of the cartridges into the chamber. He then places the muzzle against his head and pulls the trigger. At stake is one man's life. Even if nuclear war is unlikely but reasonably possible, our government's failure to shelter and shield the American people from nuclear bombs and missiles is playing Russian roulette for a hundred million American lives.

The shield was employed from the dawn of organized warfare. As knowledge grew, soldiers and noncombatants sought further protection behind city walls. In present conventional war foxholes and forts testify that temporary and durable shelters are still useful. In preparing for nuclear war, however, we have abandoned shield and shelter.

This is remarkable because we have forsworn a first nuclear strike against the USSR unless it starts a conventional war in Europe without making a first nuclear strike against the United States. Thus, if a Soviet-American nuclear war comes, we plan to bear the first blow without shelter and shield at the cost of 100,000,000-160,000,000 American lives.

Despite the millions of words spoken and written about "national defense," we have none against nuclear war, the only war that threatens our survival. Before nuclear weapons, professional officers, having studied the history of war, believed that sooner or later they would fight in one. They prepared by teaching soldiers to dig in as well as to shoot. It is amazing, therefore, that with our civilian population already the target of nuclear weapons, politicians and the military have devoted little thought to shelter.

Active defense, if we had it, would strive to prevent enemy missiles from striking the United States. Civil defense, though sometimes called passive, is anything but; it requires active preparation, training, and execution. Civil defense is passive, however, in the sense that it only shelters. It is not aggressive; it saves lives, mitigates property damage, and preserves.

The history of our civil defense since 1947 is the story of a small devoted band of men and women battering in vain against a wall of official inertia. Our states and cities have been more troubled about our lack of shelter than our presidents or Congress. Except John F. Kennedy, inspired by the 1962 Cuban missile crisis, no president has had a strong commitment to civil defense. Presidential budget requests, varying from large to small, have been cut heavily by Congress without a strong effort by the president to restore them. The military establishment has been so enamored by its effort to increase the strength of our deterrent that it has had slight sympathy with shelter. Although some secretaries of defense have paid lip service to American civil defense to offset Soviet civil defense, their small requested appropriations for civil defense have belied their words.

We have made a token effort. Since 1951 we have spent over $2 billion on civil defense. Most of the money has gone into overhead, salaries, research, testing shelters, and the like. W.E. Strope, consultant on civil defense at the Stanford Research Institute, told an instructive anecdote: The Naval Radiological Defense Laboratory built a demonstration civil defense shelter with fluted steel walls. Strope saw a visitor rubbing his hands over the corrugations on the steel and asked him why. He replied: "I've been in civil defense since it was invented in 1950, and this is the first thing I've been able to touch that wasn't paper."[1]

Although we have some public shelters in large cities, few Americans know the location of their nearest one. Some of our

1. W. E. Strope, House Armed Services Committee, *Civil Defense Review*, H.A.S.C. No. 94-421, U. S. Government Printing Office, Washington, 1976, p. 338.

money has been wasted. Some has gone into preparation for natural disasters, which has proved its worth in emergencies. While we have little tangible to show for our expenditures, we have acquired some valuable intangibles that can be translated into tangibles: We have good liaison between our Defense Civil Preparedness Agency (now Federal Emergency Management Agency) and local governmental authorities. Through research and experiments we know what to do. And we have developed an excellent team of professional experts to direct a program if and when the money to do so is available.

To put effective American civil defense into operation will require a large sum. In 1973 our Defense Civil Preparedness Agency prepared a report based on the 1973 Post Nuclear Attack Study (PONAST II) made for the Joint Chiefs of Staff by an interagency group, including the major defense and intelligence agencies and 22 federal civilian agencies. Accurately summarizing the report in 1975, Senator Howard Baker (Tennessee) said that we could reduce our fatalities from a Soviet surprise nuclear attack to 5 or 6 percent of our population by spending about $35 billion.[2] But the dollar has shrunk, and probably the estimate is too low; $50 billion to $100 billion is nearer the mark. The aggregate sum misleads. The Soviets have been spending more than $4 per capita per year; the Swiss $11; the United States about 40 cents. To catch up we must spend more than the Swiss per person. If we do, we can cut our casualties to a bearable proportion. Is $25 per person per year too much to pay for survival?

The obvious need to start full-scale American civil defense has become clouded by the argument in its favor based on the effective Soviet civil defense. Even if the USSR had no civil defense, the reason for beginning and completing our civil defense would be valid. Once the capability of nuclear war is granted, the debate is over. The basic case for American civil defense can be reduced to a single sentence: Civil defense can save millions of American lives.

2. *Congressional Record*, Senate, June 24, 1975, p. S11411. Although the PONAST II report is classified, an extensive briefing of it can be obtained from FEMA (Federal Emergency Management Agency), Washington, D.C.

We shall never be able to think sensibly about shelter until we stop treating nuclear war as a nightmare and posit that it may come despite deterrence. Fiction and drama have portrayed a bleak vision of the destruction of the human race by nuclear war. The writers are not to blame; they are bolstered by our official assertions. Henry Kissinger told the Senate Foreign Relations Committee: "Each side has the capacity to destroy civilization as we know it." His successor Cyrus Vance echoed: "A nuclear war would result in the destruction of the world as we know it."[3] The media have gone farther; "extinction of the human species" is a typical statement. The exaggeration is apparent; a Soviet-American war would leave most of the world unharmed except for deaths from fallout that would kill some but not wipe out populations or civilization.

French deaths and destruction of property in World War I were very large proportionately; France recovered. In World War II the Germans inflicted tremendous casualties and devastation on the USSR; it emerged a superpower.

If the Japanese had had basements in Hiroshima and Nagasaki and even a short warning of the atomic attacks, the number of casualties would have been sharply reduced. The next day after the blast in Hiroshima the bridges were open to traffic; the second day trains were operating; the third day some streetcar lines resumed service.

Admittedly, the destruction from present nuclear weapons would be awesome. Nonetheless the bleak vision is rejected by the USSR, China, Switzerland, and Sweden, whose civil defense would hold down their fatalities from a nuclear war to bearable proportions.

An article in the April 6, 1975 *Bulletin of the Atomic Scientists* argued that with its existing stockpile of nuclear missiles the United States could destroy the world's population "twelve times over." In refuting, former American Ambassador to the USSR Foy D. Kohler noted that the author's result was reached by multiplying the casualties per kiloton in Hiroshima and Nagasaki by the total number of kilotons possessed by the United States and

3. H. Kissinger, Department of State *Bulletin,* October 14, 1974, v. 71, No. 1842, p. 512; C. Vance, ibid., July 18, 1977, No. 1986, p. 88.

then dividing by the number of people in the world. Such a calculation does not consider how many of our weapons would survive a Soviet attack on us or how many of the rest could deliver their missiles and warheads on target. The method also implies that the entire target population has been collected into the same density as in Hiroshima and Nagasaki and is completely unwarned. By such a method it can be proved that the world's inventory of artillery shells or even kitchen knives can kill the human population.

Experience proves the fallacy of annihilation by arithmetic. Most of the people of Germany, Japan, and Italy survived World War II despite the more than 10 billion pounds of TNT dropped on them during the war, which equalled more than 50 pounds for every man, woman, and child in the three countries. Arithmetically they all should have been dead. During the Vietnam War, more than 25 billion pounds of TNT were dumped on North and South Vietnam (by air 15 billion, by other means some 10 billion) for an average of some 730 pounds for each of a total population of 34 million and an average of 3,000 pounds for each person in prime target areas. Nonetheless, the United States was unable to kill enough people or to disrupt sufficiently to avoid a humiliating defeat.

Soviet military doctrine has never accepted the "overkill" concept prominent in American writings. Rather the Soviet emphasis has been on survivability and on victory in a nuclear war, a fact which Secretary of Defense Harold Brown has at last admitted.[4]

The fallout damage from a nuclear exchange has been grossly exaggerated. Studies of our Oak Ridge National Laboratories have shown that a simple structure that any one can build with mostly earth and water will protect a person against very strong fallout for a period of from eight to ten days, by which time the fallout will have lost its danger. In the Congressional civil defense hearings of 1976, Conrad V. Chester of Oak Ridge National Laboratories, a recognized expert in his field, testified:

4. F. D. Kohler, Foreword to L. Gouré, *War Survival in Soviet Strategy*, Center for Advanced International Studies, University of Miami, Washington, 1976, pp. xiv-xv; *Annual Defense Department Report* FY 1981, pp. 38, 82-83.

The movie, "On the Beach," produced in many . . . American minds the image of nuclear war in which every human in the world was doomed by worldwide fallout. . . . We have looked closely at the effects in the United States. Under the rather pessimistic assumption that a Soviet force of over 5,000 megatons was ground burst, we found that the most serious long-term radiological problem was contamination of cropland by strontium-90. The long-term effect of this contamination could be an increase of 30 percent in cancer incidence in some parts of the country, again occurring about 15 years after the attack. While this increase is undesirable, it does not threaten national survival. It could be canceled out by neglecting to rebuild the cigarette industry.[5]

Chester also noted Oak Ridge's demonstration by experiment that expedient shelters can be built with materials easily available.

Chester's appraisal may be too optimistic. Because there can be no trial and error except by a nuclear exchange, no prediction can be accurate. But the estimates of fallout casualties by the experts at Oak Ridge can be tripled, and still shelter would assure national survival.

The arguments against civil defense rely mostly on catchwords. Mutual assured destruction advocates contend that American civil defense would be "provocative"; if we evacuated our cities, the USSR would read the evacuation as preparation for an American first strike and would launch its missiles to gain the advantage of the first blow. But American civil defense proponents do not suggest American evacuation except in response to a previous Soviet evacuation. Even if one accepts mutual assured destruction, the doctrine does not apply to civil defense, which both the USSR and China practice, and which neither comprehends why we do not copy. In puzzlement Chou En-lai (Zxou Enlai) asked visiting American Congressmen why the United States did not adopt the cheapest and simplest kind of defense. In 1977, 22 American civil defense directors made a short visit to Moscow and Leningrad at Soviet invitation. Their hosts could

5. C. V. Chester, *Civil Defense Review*, p. 361; see also pp. 360-368.

not understand why Americans did not regard civil defense as a basic humane necessity.[6]

Senator William Proxmire (Wisconsin), a long time foe of civil defense, says it is not cost effective. In choosing between competing offensive weapons or designs, cost effectiveness may be one of the criteria. But to debate whether a dollar spent on shelter is as cost effective as a dollar spent on deterrence is to neglect our paramount objective; for deterrence alone cannot insure our survival. We should spend enough to have both effective deterrence and shelter. Between prosperity and survival, the latter is primary.

Though our experts estimate that civil defense will reduce our fatalities from a nuclear attack to 5 or 6 percent of our population, assume they are mistaken. As Genesis relates, when the Lord was about to destroy Sodom, Abraham asked Him if He would spare the city if there were "fifty righteous . . . therein." The Lord said: "Yes." Abraham kept lowering the number until he reached 10, with the Lord still saying yes. Are not 10, yea, even five million American lives worth saving?

In 1977 Secretary of Defense Harold Brown, who learned mutual assured destruction under former Secrtetary of Defense Robert S. McNamara, said of Soviet evacuation doctrine:

> In case of a presumed threat of nuclear war they are supposed to start walking out into the countryisde. . . .
> If they keep on building up a civil defense capability, . . .
> I don't think that the way to respond is by matching their civil defense program. . . . Our appropriate response would be to modernize and bring up to date and retarget our strategic forces, and if we did that, as we would, then I think all that civil defense would have gone for nothing.[7]

T. K. Jones of Boeing Aerospace Co., an expert on civil defense, made these telling replies: To overcome the effect of observed examples of Soviet industrial dispersal could require

6. J. H. Proctor, "Five Days in Russia," *Journal of Civil Defense,* May-June 1977, v. 10, No. 3, p. 2.

7. H. Brown, National Broadcasting Company telecast *Meet the Press,* March 6, 1977, transcript pp. 2-3.

an eight-fold American increase in megatonnage. To overcome Soviet hardening measures would require a 22-fold to 43-fold increase in American warheads.[8] To raise Soviet population losses to the 20 percent level would require a six-fold increase in our weapons surviving a Soviet first strike.[9]

The answer to Brown is more fundamental than his error about retargeting or the fact that his Annual Defense Department reports have suggested no "appropriate response." The mistake is to base American civil defense on the need to respond to Soviet civil defense rather than on our need for shelter.

Brown also informs us that "civil defense . . . really is inappropriate for the nature of U. S. society."[10] He assumes that the American people are so heedless that they are determined to have no shelter from a prospective nuclear attack. The facts are exactly the reverse. Jiri Nehnevajsa of the University of Pittsburgh, a distinguished expert on public opinion polls and surveys, has assembled all of them on strategic and civil defense in a data bank. It covers a span of nearly 25 years and represents about 500 studies and about 500,000 individual respondents. He says:

> What all these data tell us is that strategic defense, especially as embodied in civil defense, has enjoyed a consistently high level of public support over the years. Few public programs command such a broad base of passive approval.[11]

The pertinent question is not whether we should have civil defense; the questions are what kind and how extensive. The best existing models help to answer.

Neither Switzerland nor Sweden has engaged in war since

8. T.K. Jones, Minority Views in Joint Committee Print,*Civil Preparedness Review, Part 2, Industrial Defense and Nuclear Attack,* U. S. Government Printing Office, Washington, 1977, p. 105. The report written by Senator William Proxmire ignored the testimony of Jones.

9. T. K. Jones, *Effect of Evacuation and Sheltering on Potential Fatalities from a Nuclear Exchange,* Boeing Aerospace Co., Seattle, August 15, 1977, p. 3.

10. H. Brown, *Meet the Press,* March 6, 1977, transcript, pp. 2-3.

11. J. Nehnevajsa, *Civil Defense Review,* p. 327; updated, *Journal of Civil Defense,* December 1979, v. 12, No. 6, p. 5.

1815; neither has nuclear weapons; neither is an aggressive nation. They are far less likely victims of a nuclear attack than the United States, but they continue to take steps to protect their populations, for in the words of the 1969 Swiss Civil Defense Handbook: "The idea of perpetual peace is attractive but there is nothing to indicate that we have made one step toward it." By 1975 the 6,520,000 Swiss had 2,500,000 shelter spaces which protect against blast, heat, radiation, building collapse, and biological and chemical warfare. By 1978 Switzerland had provided 4,000,000 perfect, modern shelter places, fully protected and air-conditioned. By 1975 Switzerland had also provided additional excellent, though not as good, shelter for another 1,800,000 people. Since 1975 the Swiss have added hardened underground tunnels, stocked with food, and containing complete hospitals. Every Swiss male citizen not in military service must serve in civil defense; reserves discharged from military service at age 50 have to serve in civil defense until age 60. The Swiss program is steady, combining all elements; by 2000 the Swiss will be able to protect their entire population.

In Sweden it is commonplace to find schools, garages, hangars, factories, power plants, emergency operating centers, and the like under granite shields of fifty feet or more. By 1975, for 8 million inhabitants Sweden had provided 5 million shelter spaces; by the turn of the century there will be between 11 million and 12 million such spaces to protect the Swedish people at home and at work.

The large western democracies are supposed to be among the advanced nations. Not in civil defense. Britain, which proved the effectiveness of damage control in World War II, has practically none now.

The Chinese proudly display their tunnels. On his 1975 visit to them, Doctor Ishwar Ojha, a political scientist of Boston University, was amazed:

> So they took us to the busiest marketing section of Peking and into a large department store. And on one counter they pressed a button; the counter rolled away, and we saw steps leading down. We went down about eight meters, about 28 feet, and found tunnels, all right

— well-built brick and concrete tunnels, miles and miles of them. The entire city of Peking, they told us, has tunnels under it, with an entrance from every department store, every apartment building, every residence. Inside the tunnels we saw kitchens, running water, sanitary facilities, food storage, medical facilities, all ready for use. In the event of a nuclear attack, they said, Peking's 7 million people can be safe in the tunnels in seven minutes, and can walk through them to 20 miles outside the city. And they told us that, since 1968, every major city in China had had similar tunnels built. So whenever we went to another city, we asked to see the tunnels — and they were there.[12]

American Congressmen have inspected the Chinese tunnels and confirmed.

We know much about the Soviet model. The Civil Defense Panel of the Subcommittee on Investigations of the House Committee on Armed Services conducted public hearings in 1976 and printed the evidence taken in a report.[13] This was the first time the Committee had examined the full range of civil defense operations under our Civil Defense Act of 1950 in over a decade. The hearings received scant attention in the media, but Soviet observers attended all sessions. Professor Leon Gouré studied Soviet civil defense as a senior analyst for the Rand Corporation (1951-1969), and has carried on his work with the Center for Advanced International Studies, University of Miami. In 1976 he published the definitive work on his subject.[14] The account of Soviet civil defense which follows is based on the House hearings, Gouré's work, numerous publications of our Oak Ridge National Laboratory operated by Union Carbide for our Atomic Energy Committee, publications of our Defense Civil Preparedness Agency, plus Soviet and American literature on the subject, including Defense Department reports and posture statements by the Joint Chiefs of Staff.

12. I. Ojha, *Survive*, January-February 1975, v. 8, No. 1, p. 1.

13. House Armed Services Committee, *Civil Defense Review*.

14. L. Gouré, *War Survival in Soviet Strategy*.

The USSR asserts that only a nation which fails to protect itself by civil defense will suffer unbearable casualties in a nuclear war. The practice of the USSR has corresponded; it has a large comprehensive war survival program, which celebrated it forty-seventh birthday in 1979. Soviet civil defense is headed by a deputy minister of defense, commanded by a colonel general, and ranked as a major branch of the armed services. Massive propaganda prepares the people for the dangers of nuclear war and attempts to persuade them that such a war will not mean the destruction of their homeland. The propaganda is also designed to convince them that the USSR will be the victor. Training in civil defense for men (16-60) and for women (16-55) is compulsory. Since the mid-1950s seven courses totaling 124 hours of training time have been given to the entire people. The basic course of 20 hours, started in 1973, is raised to 28-30 hours for members of civil defense formations, 36-44 hours for unit leaders, and 70-90 hours for command staff personnel. In addition all must participate in various exercises. School children are taught civil defense in the second, fifth, and ninth grades for a total of 57 hours. In Pioneer summer camps and in the national war games program, in which 16 million to 20 million Soviet children participate annually, they receive additional training. Vocational and technical schools and colleges provide further instruction.

The Soviet leaders emphasize civil defense work as a patriotic duty. Still there has been some degree of public apathy and official bumbling; there always is. The program has moved from scholastic to practical training, including preparation for evacuation, construction of hasty fallout shelters, medical self-help, and first aid.

To protect against inhalation, ingestion, or skin contact with radioactive fallout and chemical agents, the USSR manufactures gas masks for children and adults, gas bags for infants, protective clothing, medical kits, and the like, fully distributed to civil defense personnel and generally to the working population.

The Soviet program relies heavily on preattack evacuation of the urban population to preassigned prepared rural locations, and Soviet manuals suggest that evacuation will be complete in 72 hours, which is within Soviet transport capability. Since 1974, however, the authorities have sought to speed up evacuation; the younger workers and residents are to walk out of the cities. Such evacuations have been practiced in factory exercises.

In the second half of the 1950s Soviet hardened shelter construction began in factories, public buildings, and apartment buildings; ten years later the Soviets decided because of expense to continue such shelter construction only at industrial sites and new public buildings. But in 1974 a shift was made toward providing shelter protection for the entire population. The shelters are various: separate standing and in basements, the hasty type, and the best with double blast doors, filter ventilation systems, air regeneration systems, and other such features. The cumulative construction has provided shelter capacity for a large proportion of the population, and more shelters are being added every year. Because the population is being trained in the construction of hasty shelters, the Soviets believe that everyone should be able to obtain protection in blast or fallout shelters within 72 hours of a governmental announcement of a threatening situation. Our Oak Ridge National Laboratory constructed expedient shelters based on designs published in the USSR, which were then tested by our Defense Civil Preparedness Agency and found to be exceedingly effective.

As part of its war survival plan, the USSR believes that it can preserve and restore its essential ecomony during a nuclear war. In vital factories essential workers will remain on the job and occupy hardened shelters on the premises. All over the country food, fuel, raw materials, and spare parts have been stockpiled and protected against nuclear strikes. Amount and locations are secret, but probably the war food reserve is sufficient for a year. Though the USSR has propagandized in favor of treaties prohibiting chemical and biological warfare — without any means of verification — the Soviet program includes special alerts for such attacks.

The Soviets have fueled their doctrine with their money. They do not publish their figures, but conservative estimates put their expenditures for civil defense since they started their shelter construction at $1 billion annually, or about $4 per person per year. In 1977, when 44 American civil defense directors visited

Moscow at Soviet invitation, they were given a briefing by officials of the USSR. One of our defense directors asked about the size of the Soviet civil defense budget. The reply was: $1.35 billion per year.[15] Most of the Soviet money has gone into hardware because practically all civil defense workers are unpaid and training is conducted during free time periods. By 1976 the USSR probably had invested over $20 billion in civil defense, little of which had gone into salaries or the like. And the work goes on.

Since 1966, the Soviets have emphasized defense as well as economic considerations in the sites of their industrial plants. During the five-year plan for 1966-1970 almost 60 percent of new plants were built in small towns and cities rather than in metropolitan areas. This dispersal, however, has been somewhat offset by additions to existing factories in large cities.

How effective is Soviet civil defense? We shall never be able to answer with assurance until it is too late. No estimate on war between two opponents armed with nuclear weapons can be accurate; for there has never been one. As Fred Iklé pointed out in the speech quoted earlier, we have no experience to guide us. We do, however, have instructive estimates.

In 1968 Secretary of Defense Robert S. McNamara scaled down his previous requirements for deterring the USSR to our assured capability to destroy one-fifth to one-fourth of the Soviet population and one-half of Soviet industrial capacity.[16] If our second-strike capability lives up to expectation, and the if is large, we estimate that we can knock out 50 percent of Soviet industrial capacity, a loss which the USSR could rebuild. But because of Soviet civil defense, the Soviets calculate that their loss of life from an American second strike probably would not exceed 4 to 6 percent of their population. Their 1969 Civil Defense Manual estimated that their urban killed would be only between 5 and 8 percent of their urban population.[17] That comes to a loss of

15. Proctor, "Five Days in Russia," p. 2.

16. R. S. McNamara, *Statement to Senate Armed Services Committee on FY1969-1973 Defense Program and 1969 Defense Budget,* Department of Defense, Washington, 1968, p. 50.

17. N. I. Akimov et al., *Civil Defense,* Kolos (Heads of Grains), Moscow, 1969, translated by S. J. Rimshaw, p. 68. See also P. T. Yegerov et al., *Civil Defense,* Publishing House for Higher Education, Moscow, 1970, translated under the supervision of the U. S. Air Force, pp. 73-74.

7.5 million to 12 million people out of an urban population of 151 million. Because at the time of the calculation the USSR was still about 40 percent rural, its estimated total loss of life would have been no more than 4 to 6 percent of its total population, considerably less than its loss of 20 million lives during World War II, from which the USSR emerged as one of the two dominant powers. And the 20 million lost by the USSR during World War II was cumulative to a loss of many millions of lives during Joseph Stalin's great purge, which occurred immediately before World War II.

The Soviet statements may be false propaganda designed to strengthen the resolve of the people; the estimate of the rulers may greatly exceed 4 to 6 percent. But nations have recovered from much heavier losses; without going any further back than World War II, the USSR did. Moreover, the calculations of our experts on Soviet losses from an American second strike after an evacuation of Soviet cities confirm the 4 to 6 percent appraisal.[18] During the 1977 visit previously mentioned of our civil defense directors to Moscow, they asked a United States Embassy spokesman what Soviet civil defense was really like. He answered: "All the facts are in Gouré's book." The Russians corroborated.[19]

At long last, so do our Joint Chiefs of Staff. In 1977 Senator William Proxmire submitted a series of issues to them, and asked for their comments:

> *Issue:* That the implication [of mass shelter construction] is that they — USSR — have quietly and at extra expense taken measures to assure that the essential civilian-military leadership, the fighting capability, and the production capacity can continue to function under conditions of total war.
>
> *Comment:* The Soviet program is more extensive

18. L. Gouré, T. K. Jones, and E. P. Wigner, *Civil Defense Review*, pp. 193, 199-201, 248, 285. Our Oak Ridge Laboratory is in accord as are independent calculations by the Strategic Command U. S. Air Force.

19. Proctor, "Five Days in Russia," p. 3.

and better-developed than it appeared to be several years ago. Under optimum conditions, which include a period of warning prior to an unrestrained U. S. attack and successful evacuation and other preparations, Soviet civil-defense measures could probably: (1) assure survival of a large percentage of the leadership necessary to maintain control, (2) reduce prompt casualties among the urban population to a small percentage, and (3) give the Soviets a good chance of being able to distribute at least a subsistence level of supplies to the surviving population, although the economy as a whole would experience serious difficulties.[20]

In July 1978, Senator John C. Culver (Iowa) requested and received from our Director of Central Intelligence a report on *Soviet Civil Defense,* NI 78-10003. The report rates the Soviet effort rather highly but discounts some of the claims in its favor made by advocates of civil defense. There is internal evidence that the report is biased. The subway systems in the USSR have been designed for civil defense, particularly the Moscow subway. The report admits that 17 to 34 percent of Moscow's population could be sheltered in the subway but states: "However, we have not included subways in our estimate of total shelter capacity because the subways could be intended for evacuation and because of our uncertainty about the existence of life-support systems in the subways."

In 1978 the Joint Chiefs of Staff showed signs of full awakening. In his final report as Chairman of the Joint Chiefs of Staff, General George S. Brown differed from Secretary of Defense Harold Brown. General Brown admitted that the low priority we have given to Soviet civil defense has been a mistake that requires "a reassessment":

> The Soviet Union includes civil defense as an integral part of its overall military strategy. . . . There is little doubt about the extensive nature of the Soviet civil defense program. . . . A strong and effective civil defense program [for the United States] would complement

20. Joint Chiefs of Staff, text, quoted in *U. S. News & World Report,* February 14, 1977, v. 82, No. 6, p. 61.

and support a U. S. military effort in nuclear war by enhancing the survivability of the population and the industrial capacity of the United States, upon which the nation's defense effort depends.[21]

But nothing has been done to carry out the recommendation.

In nuclear war, as in all war, attack and defense interact, and shelter is part of defense. The comparative strength and weakness of Soviet and American civil defense affect the nuclear balance, our ability to deter, the outcome, and Soviet perception of the outcome. Thus, our lack of civil defense increases the likelihood of nuclear war.

Opponents of American civil defense claim that the harsh Russian winter climate would preclude Soviet evacuation during the long winter months. T. K. Jones replies: Evacuation is practicable on all except a few days a year. The other answer is: If the Soviets intend nuclear war, they can pick the date, and it would not be during winter.

Analysts maintain that Soviet evacuation would nullify the advantage of surprise. The Soviets, however, could cause a Sino-Soviet crisis, inform us that they were evacuating in response to it, and then strike us instead of the Chinese.

All such arguments and scenarios, however, fall into the trap of basing American civil defense on Soviet civil defense. The vital reason for American civil defense needs reiteration: Nuclear war is likely. Even if it is unlikely but reasonably possible, American civil defense is essential because it can save many millions of American lives.

To save the maximum number possible, we should follow the Swiss model of durable shelters. Evacuation is much cheaper, better than nothing, and a good, if not completely safe, plan for the USSR. But evacuation is not a safe plan for us. We are unlikely to make a surprise first strike; the USSR may, and without evacuation of its cities. Instead the Soviets may gamble that we will not respond.

The assertion that because of technical deficiencies the USSR cannot make a first strike without our receiving ample warning

21. G. S. Brown, *United States Military Posture for FY1979*, Department of Defense, Washington, 1978, pp. 39-40.

fails on three counts: The statement is based on our intelligence information that often has been mistaken in the past. The claimed Soviet technological deficiencies may be cured. The case for shelter does not rest only on today, but also on the long future.

We should have durable shelters and increase our warning capability to the maximum possible. Our experts have a tendency to write scenarios. As any officer with experience in battle knows, reality rarely corresponds. This requires that we provide shelters designed to withstand future weapons as well as existing ones, and that we take account of chemical and bacteriological attack, as well as of improvements to be expected in Soviet arms and the acquisition of nuclear weapons by other nations.

In American nuclear writing, "asymmetries" frequently are shorthand for Soviet advantages over the United States. Besides the ones the USSR has created by its efforts, some Soviet civil defense advantages are inherent in the present relative situations of the two countries. The USSR is much larger in area than the United States and far more rural; the Soviet population is hence less vulnerable. Accordingly, evacuation in the United States would be far more difficult than in the USSR. To receive the evacuees, the USSR has the rural communes previously organized for agriculture; they have not had to be formed from scratch. In contrast, we have no such mechanism, and creating one would be difficult and expensive. We are an undisciplined people; the Soviet people have grown accustomed to acting upon orders from the top. The Soviet form of government makes command and response faster and easier than in our country. Our abundance of automobiles, a seeming help, is a detriment. The Soviet people are accustomed to walking; we have become addicted to the automobile. An expert favoring evacuation should think about it while traveling out of one of our large cities during the evening rush hour, and then add the extra element of panic.

In addition to all these considerations, the difference between evacuation and counterevacuation counts heavily. Even in a crisis an American president would hesitate to order counterevacuation because of the heavy cost of stopping the economy and the consequent adverse political reaction against the president if the crisis blew over.

We should do what the Swiss have done by requiring all future construction to provide full shelter protection. In single family dwellings, however, it will be sufficient for the United States to give the money and require one such equipped house per neighborhood. In addition, we should pay the cost of altering a structure or two in each residential neighborhood. Future industrial construction should be in the country rather than the cities. We should require that work places be protected. Obvious necessities are underground food storage and medical facilities. Training in civil defense in the schools and for the adult population should be obligatory. Much of the instruction can cost no money with the cooperation of labor unions, scouts, teachers, and volunteers. A good plan will combine such voluntary work with enforced law. It would be presumptuous to specify the details. The beginning is to tell the American people the truth. They are neither fools nor heedless of their safety.

The small devoted group who for years has urged civil defense in vain may consider a Swiss type program an idle dream, but the Soviet model, though better than nothing, does not meet our need. Professor Eugene P. Wigner, Nobel Laureate in Physics in 1963, nuclear expert, and long time advocate of civil defense, is correct: We must provide durable shelters.

It is a mistake to be content with a modest increase in the budget for civil defense or even an increase to $200 million a year. If we obtain such an increase, we are likely to resume our slumber.

Because nuclear war may come sooner rather than later, a crash program seems logical but probably would be a boondoggle. Nor is it likely that the money will be voted in a single year. We must therefore content ourselves with steady spending and exertions. If we put the program in the hands of the seasoned professionals who have learned civil defense over many years, a continued civil defense appropriation of $4 billion to $5 billion a year will lower our fatalities. When completed, probably shelter will assure our national survival.

Civil defense is not enough. Despite it, our loss of life in nuclear war would be heavy; of property staggering. There is no excuse for not further ameliorating the damage by active defense. We shall become reasonably safe only when we have devised, developed, and deployed an adequate defense against nuclear weapons.

Our present abandonment of defense is a departure from our early theory and practice. When manned bombers were the only threat, we worked with Canada to defend our lives and property by an extensive system, which at its height included early warning, 122 fighter interceptor squadrons (active and reserve), 280 surface to air missile batteries, and a full command, surveillance, and communication system. We started an antiballistic missile (ABM) research and development program in the mid-1950s before Sputnik showed Soviet ability to deploy intercontinental ballistic missiles (ICBMs). The first site of our Ballistic Missile Early Warning System went into operation in 1961.

In the early 1960s, however, an increase in Soviet missile strength convinced Secretary of Defense Robert S. McNamara that an ABM "defense of our cities against a Soviet attack would be a futile waste of our resources." As he perceived it, a "nuclear-armed offensive weapon which has a 50/50 chance of destroying its target would be highly effective, but a defensive weapon with the same probability of destroying incoming warheads would be of little value."[22] In 1967 McNamara temporarily modified his attitude by suggesting modest city defenses against a possible threat from China's "primitive" nuclear capabilities. In 1969 Richard Nixon substituted Safeguard for the Sentinel ABM system primarily to protect our missile silos against Soviet attack, but not to defend our people. In 1972 we restrained ourselves from acquiring an active defense by the SALT (strategic arms limitation talks) treaty in which we buried our shield. The 1972 ABM Treaty limited each country to defense by ABMs at two sites, subsequently reduced to one. The ABM treaty has a six-month cancellation clause.

We can and should disinter our shield. At the same time, we should avail ourselves of the one year cancellation clause in the ambiguous 1967 Space Treaty.

22. R. S. McNamara, *Statement before the Senate Armed Services Committee on the fiscal year 1969-1973 Defense Program and 1969 Defense Budget,* Department of Defense, Washington, 1968, pp. 63, 42.

To justify our abandonment of defense, we invented a strategy embodied in a catchphrase — mutual assured destruction (MAD). As discussed earlier, MAD's fatal flaw lies in its ignoring the capability of nuclear war despite deterrence. Donald G. Brennan of the Hudson Institute pointed out that even if the Soviets accepted MAD, it still would be pernicious:

> In spite of our best efforts a major nuclear war could happen. . . . The Defense Department should be more concerned with assuring live Americans than dead Russians . . . . [In good morals] we should not deliberately create a system in which millions of innocent civilians would be exterminated should the system fail. The system is not *that* reliable.[23]

As their writings before and after the ABM Treaty bear witness, the Soviets continue to emphasize defense. The advocates of MAD, however, hailed the signing of the 1972 ABM Treaty by the USSR as proof of its concurrence in our theory.

Soviet deeds since contradict. In 1972 the Soviets were far behind us in ABM technology. Probably they thought the treaty would allow them to catch up. It has. While we slackened our research, they accelerated theirs, until now the question is whether they have caught up or are ahead. By the treaty each side was permitted ABM defense at one site. Our one has been dismantled pursuant to a statute passed by Congress; the Soviets have developed their site in and around Moscow.

In 1980 Secretary of Defense Brown noted that the USSR has only 64 GALOSH missile launchers in and around Moscow, though the ABM Treaty permits 100. There also is an indication that the USSR will dismantle half of the 64. This offers us no comfort; for in the testing area of the Soviets, they have been diligently working on an improved ABM, not to mention that they have 2600 interceptors plus 10,000 SAM launchers accomodating 12,000 missiles.

With impeccable logic we reasoned that because we had no defense against Soviet missiles launched from land and sea, it was a waste of money to have defense against air bombard-

23. D. G. Brennan, "When the Salt Hit the Fan," *National Review,* June 23, 1972, v. 24, No. 24, p. 689.

ment. Consequently, we stripped the United States of any air defense. Since 1972, the Soviets have greatly strengthened their air defense. Testing at designated test sites was allowed by the treaty. We did little until 1976; the Soviets have done much. Whether the Soviets have violated the treaty is in dispute, but there is no dispute that they have pushed the treaty's language to its outer limits. If mutual assured destruction were indeed a shared doctrine, Soviet actions would have shattered the spirit of the ABM pact.

Since 1972, we have almost totally neglected our civil defense. While the Soviet civil defense program is an old one, an upsurge in it has occurred since 1972. The ABM Treaty was part of détente. Under its soothing influence the Soviets probably expected us to relax our efforts. We have. Since 1972, we have regarded offensive weapons as "bargaining chips" for future negotiations. This attitude has restricted our weapons development, while the Soviets have greatly expanded theirs. The Soviets may have made another estimate based on their knowledge of how our Defense Department functions. In the competition for dollars, research for a weapons system we are prohibited by treaty from deploying is bound to suffer against research and development for systems we intend to deploy. That too has come true. During the administration of Gerald Ford, Defense Department reports began to show concern about Soviet ABM development, but the appropriations requested were modest. Secretary of Defense Brown's annual reports to Congress for fiscal years 1979, 1980, and 1981 have not changed the pattern except for less concern.

McNamara's cost effectiveness, of which Jimmy Carter became an enthusiastic devotee, is another catchphrase that haunts us. It cannot be too often repeated that between defense and offense, cost effectiveness is a semantic trap; for offensive weapons cannot assure our survival.

It is fruitless to blame. We are where we are, and we cannot pour spilt milk back into the bottle. We need a reappraisal based on the necessity to preserve not only our deterrent offensive weapons, but also the lives and property of the American people by an active defense against nuclear missiles and bombs.

Because of the initial success of Adolf Hitler's blitzkrieg, our military doctrine has somewhat underrated defense in conventional war. Karl von Clausewitz is often mentioned as the father of the superiority of offense. He is cited frequently but seldom read. More than one-third of Clausewitz *On War* is devoted to defense, and he asserted: "The defensive *is the stronger form of making war*." His classic sentences sum up: "What is the conception of defense? The warding off of a blow. . . .What is the object of defense? *To preserve*."[24]

Besides increased destructiveness, nuclear war has two significant differences from conventional war. The first blow gives an enormous advantage to the attacker, of which we could only take advantage by a first strike that would be unconscionable and foolhardy. The other distinction makes nuclear defense difficult. In conventional land war, aside from counterbattery fire, the defensive fire is against advancing infantry and tanks. In nuclear war, to ward off the blow to our people, we must ward off the bombs and missiles. This task is further complicated by the triad of offensive missiles launched from land, sea, and air. Accordingly, the contention that nuclear defense is impossible has prevailed in our practice.

Before anyone makes the "impossible" argument, he should be sobered by the experience of Doctor Vannevar Bush, one time President of the Massachusetts Institute of Technology and the science advisor to Dwight D. Eisenhower. On the eve of the ICBM Bush said that it was technically impossible. During the Eisenhower administration an assortment of scientists also told us that the human system could not survive manned spaceflight.

To ward off the nuclear blow, active defense seeks to stop, deflect, or destroy the incoming missiles. To be totally effective it must neutralize all of them; to be partially effective some of them.

From 1956 to 1972 our defense was a second-grade effort in dollars spent. There were reasons for our attitude. Nuclear defense is difficult. We have not yet succeeded in our scientific efforts to detect and locate submarines. Decoys and mobile land-

24. K. von Clausewitz, *On War*, Book 6, Ch. 1.

based missiles present other problems. And eventually we may have to defend against an attack from space.

The idea of hitting a bullet with a bullet had never been tried in conventional war, but was accomplished over Kwajalen in 1962 by an ABM intercept of an ICBM launched from our Vandenberg base in California. Despite our starvation of defense, we had made significant progress before 1972. In reviewing our efforts, Charles Benson said in 1971:

> America needs a means of suppressing ballistic missile attack: 1) regardless of point of origin; 2) without detonating nuclear warheads, defensive or offensive, within the atmosphere, or at least cutting such detonation to a minimum; 3) without otherwise causing heavy local fallout in the case of high altitude detonations; 4) capable of being applied against satellite-borne bombs as well as missiles; 5) nonsaturable by MIRV and decoy attack; 6) capable of defending itself, or being defended. The technology is either available or on the verge of being available to accomplish these objectives if the resources are committed to them.[25]

Benson reviewed existing technology and his projected multiple independent missile interceptor to make a persuasive case that we can realize the goals he set.

Advanced technology suggests that the optimum may be achieved. In 1976 the Congressional Research Service issued its report on *United States and Soviet City Defenses,* prepared by John C. Collins, Senior Specialist in National Defense. While conceding the technological difficulties, the report concludes that a combination of systems has a good chance to provide adequate active defense.[26] The Collins and other reports indicate that the ultimate defense may be in space, but for space defense we must cancel the ABM and Space Treaties — as we should — for they not only stop deployment of a defense, but also severely hamper development.

25. C. Benson, "Deterrence through Defense," *National Review,* March 9, 1971, v. 23, No. 9, p. 254.

26. J. M. Collins, *United States and Soviet City Defense,* 94th Congress, 2nd Session, Senate, No. 94-268, U. S. Government Printing Office, Washington, 1976.

In 1976 a controversy inside the Defense Department became public. When he was chief of Air Force intelligence, Major General George Keegan had surrounded himself with a group of physicists whose findings — based on their own experiments — about advanced Soviet physics had been quietly interred by our Central Intelligence Agency. Upon his retirement Keegan spoke out. One of his subjects was the charged particle beam weapon. Keegan believes the Soviets may complete its development in the 1980s to neutralize all our offensive nuclear weapons. In 1976, some senior defense officials, worried about their country's fate, gave more facts to *Aviation Week & Space Technology,* which published a series of articles.

A charged particle beam weapon focuses and projects atomic particles at the speed of light and is capable of being directed into space from ground-based sites to intercept and neutralize reentry vehicles. The weapon could also be placed on spacecraft for intercepting warheads in space, thus avoiding problems in propagating the beam through the earth's atmosphere. High energy laser is part of a related technology. Our scientists call the weapons of the whole group directed-energy weapons. A number of American analysts believe that directed-energy weapons are nearing prototype testing in the USSR. Some American high energy physicists have reversed themselves and now admit that the Soviets have a program that could produce a directed-energy weapon. In 1975 Soviet physicist L. I. Rudakov visited our Lawrence Livermore Laboratory in California. From his disclosures it became apparent that the Soviet Union is also far ahead of us in controlled fusion by inertial confinement — compression of small pellets of thermal nuclear fuel — and weapons based on that technology.

At long last we have begun to extend our research, but the directors in the field have complained of hampering. In 1978 some members of Congress urged the Defense Department to speed up the Army's ballistic missile defense program at Huntsville, Alabama. The Army is becoming more optimistic about success, and the technology is rapidly changing. We are doing some preliminary testing in the laser field at White Sands missile range in New Mexico.

Soviet achievements in physics would have delighted V. I. Lenin and should concern the most enthusiastic assured destruction supporters. If the USSR perfects a defensive weapon that neutralizes all our offensive triad before we do, the Soviet word will not be check; it will be checkmate.

No expert, much less any layman, can predict the eventual nature of an adequate defense, which may not be ABMs. Senator Malcolm Wallop (Wyoming) argues persuasively that in time space-based battle stations employing laser beams can destroy all Soviet missiles, while in the meantime lower orbiting laser beam stations can do the same. With an all-out effort, he maintains, the lower orbiting stations could be operative before the end of the 1980s. Such laser stations would not be killers of human beings; they would be killers of mass destructive weapons. And they would be able to defend themselves.

Before the fact, no one can positively prove that defense is possible, but to claim that an adequate defense is impossible denies experience. Throughout the history of war, attack and defense have balanced each other.

Prudence does not exclude imagination; true prudence requires it. For creating a defense against nuclear weapons, we have suffered from a scarcity among our practical men of the creative imagination of the poet, the science-fiction writer, and of the innovative scientist.

Consider all the wonders come true at which practical men initially scoffed. Had a prediction been made in 1935 that ten years later, as the last act of World War II, the United States would drop atom bombs on Japan, how much credence would have been given to the forecast? Do not forget the mocking laughter about the "crazy" idea of the Wright brothers about a flying machine. Remember Jules Verne. Ponder two events within recent memory. After Pearl Harbor, Franklin D. Roosevelt had the vision to undertake building ships by assembly lines, which produced vessels at a rate theretofore held impossible. The science and technology by which we put men on the moon were indeed marvelous, but the creative imagination of President John F. Kennedy deserves equal credit.

A basic reason predicts the eventual success of a defense

against nuclear weapons: If men were bright enough to invent nuclear weapons, experience predicts that given the necessary resources in money and with encouragement, men will be bright enough to invent a defense. In its sweeping generality, this statement sounds like an argument advanced by advocates of world government: The world state is necessary, and since it is necessary, it is possible. The distinction lies in the contrast between the small progress men have made spiritually and the great progress men have made materially. Until men become angels, the world government conclusion is a non sequitur. But since men have conquered space, the conclusion that men can invent an adequate defense to nuclear weapons is not only possible, but probable.

The pattern of rapid change of weapons predicts that even if a good defense against today's nuclear weapons is discovered, the defense may become ineffective because of advances in science and technology. But change also applies to offensive weapons. We must have them in existence, but we need constant research and development to alter or supplant them. The same is true of defensive weapons, which we first slighted and then attempted to abolish.

For nuclear war our Department of Defense is misnamed; it has become our department of deterrence and counterattack. If nuclear war comes, however, counterattack will not bring 100,000,000-160,000,000 Americans back to life. Prudence and creative imagination counsel cancellation of the ABM treaty and the ambiguous Space Treaty and our utmost endeavor to develop and deploy a nuclear defense. To justify, it is not essential to rely on the appraisal of Keegan or any one else. The reason goes deeper: For our primary aim of survival, defense offers the best chance.

CHAPTER 4

Supposed Tools of Peace

Our era differs from all those gone before because with our present lack of defense nuclear war can kill at least half of us. So realizing, the question is not whether we want nuclear peace; practically all of us do. The pertinent question is: By what tool can we best keep the peace?

The two tools most commonly associated with peace are diplomacy and treaties. The fruit of diplomacy is a treaty; logically therefore diplomacy comes first. But because the tree must be judged by the fruit it bears, starting with treaties is more instructive.

Such useful pacts as those about copyright, safety at sea, extradition, and a host of other subjects may be eliminated as not of great moment in the life of our nation. The operation to be observed is of treaties about war or peace.

Labels work magic. Because of them, subconsciously we associate treaties with peace and their absence with war. Yet throughout history treaties and war have comfortably coexisted.

In his 1977 Inaugural Address President Jimmy Carter said: "We will move this year a step toward our ultimate goal: the elimination of all nuclear weapons from this earth." Had Carter been asked "by what tool," his reply would have had to be: by international law or treaty. International law comprises treaties and the customs of so-called civilized nations. Custom is more uncertain than treaties, and international law has been violated as often as treaties. The reply can therefore be shortened to treaties.

In his daily Bible reading, Carter must have skipped the 34th chapter of Genesis, which relates the negotiation of a disarmament treaty and its consequences. Jacob bought land and camped in the land of the Hivites. After their Prince Shechem saw Dinah, Jacob's daughter, "and lay with her, and defiled her," Shechem and his father King Hamor met with Jacob's sons and offered marriage, any gift asked, the sharing of the Hivite land, and intermarriage among the two peoples so that they would become one. Jacob's sons agreed on condition that all the male Hivites be circumcised. In urging ratification of the treaty, Hamor and Shechem told their people: "These men *are* peaceable with us." The Hivites accepted the condition, and their males were circumcised.

Immediately after the mass circumcision, the sons of Jacob, having in effect disarmed the Hivites by temporarily disabling their men pursuant to the treaty, fell upon them, slew the males, spoiled the city, and seized the women, children, and cattle. The disease that killed the Hivites was treaty reliance. The treaty on which they had relied had disarmed them.

From earliest times to the present, the history of political treaties has been a dreary repetition of breaches. *The Federalist* (No. 15) relates "how little dependence is to be placed on treaties." V. I. Lenin ridiculed those who supposed treaties would be performed. Although the first rule of treaties has been that all nations have habitually broken them, in its short history the USSR has become the champion treaty breaker.

Unreliable treaties become more untrustworthy with such a partner. If John Doe told his friends that he intended to risk all his worldly goods in a poker game with a known cardsharp, the friends would shake their heads. Yet we consider ourselves sagacious in staking our survival on treaties with the USSR, whose ideology blesses cheating as a virtue.

To sophisticates the discussion of the undependability of treaties may seem elucidation of the obvious. But those bitten by the bug of treaty reliance have been not only idealists or politicians unaware of the habitual duplicity of governments; during modern history (1500-), many sophisticated statesmen have been caught in the treaty trap. Reliance is evident from actions. Louis XIV of France, who broke treaties regularly, wrote a memoir for the guidance of his heirs in which he told them that a treaty between rivals would be broken and advised them to do likewise.

Yet again and again Louis was caught with his guard down from reliance on treaties. Frederick the Great took pernicious pleasure in breaking his alliance pacts, but when Britain broke a treaty with the double-dealing Prussian, Frederick was outraged and hated England to the end of his days. From 1939 until Adolf Hitler attacked the USSR in 1941, Joseph Stalin shredded many treaties but still relied on his pact with Hitler, as is apparent from the fact that Stalin was surprised by the German assault.

When the Soviet Union and four other communist-ruled nations invaded Czechoslovakia in August 1968, thereby each violated the multilateral United Nations treaty to keep the peace and the multilateral Warsaw Pact alliance. Each of the five invading nations also broke a bilateral alliance treaty with Czechoslovakia. Seven solemn treaties were torn up by the invasion; the number of breaches was 15. Two months later, Richard M. Nixon and Hubert H. Humphrey, the two major candidates for president of the United States, each pledged that he would request the Senate to give its consent to the Nuclear Nonproliferation Treaty of which the Soviet Union was a prominent signatory. The Senate did, though Leonid Brezhnev had reaffirmed Lenin's affirmation that it is a duty to break treaties to advance communism.

The second rule of treaties is: Treaty-reliance has been an occupational disease of statesmen. Every future treaty will be subject to this infirmity.

The third rule of treaties reveals their additional deficiency as a tool to keep the peace: Behind private contracts stands the ultimate enforcement power of the sheriff; among nations there is no sheriff. Against a country that breaks a treaty of great moment, the only effective remedy is war.

Two, and only two, types of treaties have been of some use in keeping the peace despite their unreliability. The most effective kind for this purpose has been treaties for mutual aid in war, defensive alliances. And offensive alliance treaties sometimes have served their intended objectives despite habitual breach.

The story of alliance treaties displays nations at their worst, grasping and perfidious. But notwithstanding their wretched history, alliance pacts have been the most useful type. Often the ally deserted during war, but the soldiers it furnished helped while they fought. Such treaties to aid in war, when defensive, have been the most effective to deter attack. The aggressive opponent may have guessed that the defensive coalition would dissolve under assault but could not be certain if and when defections would occur. Charles de Gaulle was sure that the United States would not risk its own nuclear devastation in the event of a Soviet attack in Europe, and many other Europeans, as well as Americans, have expressed doubt, but the Soviets cannot be certain. Hence, for our European allies the North Atlantic Treaty has worth.

The most common type of treaties to preserve peace have been peace treaties closing wars. They have been useful for specifying the conveyances of territory and other agreed terms, but have been regularly overturned when one of the signatories believed it could benefit thereby and thought it was strong enough to wage war. The most useless part of such treaties has been their promises of future peace. Nonetheless, settlement treaties, including those closing wars, have not been wholly ineffectual. Sometimes they have delayed wars or even prevented them for a considerable number of years, a worthwhile achievement.

The best illustration is the 1878 settlement Treaty of Berlin, whose story is not fit for children at bedtime. It is a tale of treaties riddled by breach, of treachery to allies, and of deceit by the great European powers. The settlement treaty itself robbed Turkey of territory the great powers had guaranteed to protect. As a consolation prize, Turkey received from all the great powers a new guarantee of such territory as Turkey had left. In violation of its promise, each of the guarantors then looted the Turkish Empire; though made "in the name of Almighty God," no treaty has been so systematically shattered as the Treaty of Berlin.

That, however, is not the moral of this story. Because the great powers profited by Turkey's losses, a war of England and Austria-Hungary against Russia did not occur. As time went on, England, France, and Russia became more afraid of Germany and Austria-Hungary than of each other. Alas for ethics; how do the wicked flourish.

The basics of treaties are: habitual breach, treaty reliance, and war as the only effective means of redressing a violation of moment. These scarcely recommend treaties as a tool for keeping the peace or for our survival with the possible exception of defensive alliances and temporary settlement treaties. Any benefit from such treaties must be balanced against expected breach and the risks of treaty-reliance.

If the treaty fruit is rotten, can the diplomatic tree be better? It is possible; for in addition to its role in negotiating treaties, diplomacy is the messenger among nations.

A high regard for one's own profession is natural. It is hardly astonishing then that the eminent practitioners and students of diplomacy Henry A. Kissinger, George F. Kennan, and Hans J. Morgenthau agree on one point: They exalt diplomacy as our tool of choice for peace.

Diplomacy's pace has quickened. When General Andrew Jackson defeated the British redcoats at New Orleans in January 1815, he was unaware that a British-American peace treaty had been signed 15 days before at Ghent. News of Jackson's victory and of the treaty reached Washington almost simultaneously; nowadays we have a hotline to Moscow. But save for increased celerity, diplomacy has not changed its ancient lineaments.

During Harry Truman's second presidental term, the Republicans dubbed our State Department "Foggy Bottom" and its denizens "cookie pushers." The skill, wit, and ebullience of Henry Kissinger lifted the man and his profession to star status. And by shrewdly identifying diplomacy as the instrument of peace, Kissinger raised in popular esteem a tool stained by habitual chicanery.

It is not only the tale of broken treaties that so testifies; diplomatic assurances have been as untrustworthy as the pacts diplomacy has created. In his excellent history of European diplomacy, David Jayne Hill relates and sometimes deplores the deceit that marked diplomacy until 1775 when his story ended. Had he gone on, the record would have been no different.

The communists have more than conformed. Good communists believe that misrepresentation to advance their "holy" cause is moral. The Soviets applied this precept in 1962 when they lied to President John F. Kennedy about their missiles in Cuba.

It is unfair to heap the blame on the diplomats. When a diplomat has lied for his country, usually he has been merely carrying out the orders of his political superiors. Louis XI of France (1423-1483) instructed his emissaries: "If they lie to you, see to it that you lie much more to them." Though American and noncommunist European diplomats have been mostly honorable since World War II, the ethical record of the western democracies still has numerous stains. While we were preparing the armed band for the 1961 Cuban invasion, the Cuban foreign minister charged us with so doing and appealed to the United Nations. In appearances before its Security Council our representatives flatly and falsely denied the charge. Moreover, they represented to the Security Council and to Cuba that we were upholding the very treaties which we were violating. If our representatives did not know that their statements were false, President Dwight D. Eisenhower did.

It follows that a healthy distrust of not only communist, but also of all, diplomatic assurances is sensible. It does not follow that we should dispense with diplomacy; for despite its shabby ethics, diplomacy has accomplished much. The domain of the United States was vastly expanded by the skillful bargaining of our peace commissioners in the negotiations ending our Revolutionary War, by Thomas Jefferson's Louisiana Purchase, and by Secretary of State William H. Seward's 1867 purchase of Alaska from Russia. Nor has diplomacy been useless for peace. The art has been at its best in finding a formula for compromise between nations that did not want to fight. This was evident in the 1846 British-American settlement of our northwestern boundary with Canada. The British three times proposed arbitration, and President James K. Polk found expansion south at the expense of Mexico easier than war with a formidable British foe.

Conciliatory diplomacy, however, cannot stop a government determined to go to war; Adolf Hitler could not be appeased. And when the message has been a warning or an ultimatum, diplomacy has been only the messenger; relative armed might has called the turn. In spite of diplomacy's formal conventions, Charles de Gaulle was correct: Diplomacy recognizes only realities.[1]

1. C. de Gaulle, *The War Memoirs of Charles de Gaulle*, v. 2, Simon and Schuster, New York, 1959, p. 211.

One of the slogans used to underpin our policy of détente has been: It is better to talk than fight, or as Winston S. Churchill previously had put it, to jaw-jaw rather than to war-war. Obviously Churchill did not believe his aphorism covered all cases; both in 1914 and 1939 he was for war-war. The short answer to the slogan is: Sometimes. After Pearl Harbor, it was better to fight. But it has been common to talk and fight at the same time. Conversation to lull an adversary into a false sense of security has been a standard diplomatic booby trap. With malice aforethought the British ambassador was still negotiating at Madrid in 1804 while the British fleet was seizing the Spanish treasure ships on the high seas. In 1941 the Japanese attacked Pearl Harbor while their envoy was parleying in Washington.

During the euphoria attendant upon Richard Nixon's 1972 journeys — the beginning of détente — the frequency of the utterance by commentators of "better talk than fight," prompted a calculation. Because between nations talk is diplomacy, while fighting is war, "better talk than fight" appropriately is transmuted to: Diplomacy avoids war. France is the mother of diplomacy. From 1500 through 1972 France maintained steady diplomatic relations with all European countries except nations with which it was at war, and even then negotiations often continued. For the 473 years France was at war with a European nation during approximately 42 percent of the years in question. If wars with other nations had been counted, the percentage would have been much higher.

Intense French diplomatic intercourse with other European nations did not cause the frequent wars with them, but the diplomatic intercourse and the frequent wars coexisted. The vice in the slogan is its implication that nations that talk together will not fight.

In essence diplomacy has been and is a patching tool for the short term. For that purpose, the praise of such brilliant expositors as Kennan, Kissinger, and Morgenthau is warranted. The diplomats who averted a general European war in 1905-1906, 1908-1909, and 1911 performed well; that they failed in 1914 was tragic. War becomes necessary only when there is no alternative;

the diplomats who seek to spare their countries from war follow an honorable calling.

The limitation of diplomacy is that it does not, and in most cases cannot, follow through. The final 1832 treaty "settling" the Greek War of Independence provided:

> The undersigned Plenipotentiaries of the Three Courts [Great Britain, France, and Russia],... declare ... that the prolonged negotiations to which those stipulations have given rise, are terminated in such a manner as never to be renewed; in fact the Greek question is irrevocably settled.

Ever since 1832, the boundaries of Greece, which the diplomats thought they had settled, have been unsettled by war and subversion. The supposedly tied game between Greece and its neighbors did not stay tied.

Sometimes diplomacy has averted a war; more often than not it has failed. Diplomacy remains an indispensable tool of statecraft, but because one American nuclear war can be fatal, the limitations of diplomacy disqualify the tool to accomplish our paramount aim of survival. This becomes apparent from the simple pattern of treaties, diplomacy, and war throughout history. Treaties have not kept the peace, and the tree is no better than its fruit. Diplomacy has been practiced as long as war. If diplomacy were capable of preventing war, the history of nations would not have been a history of war.

Without heed to this lesson, politicians and diplomats laud the balance of power as the preferred method to preserve peace. In theory no nation will start a war unless the odds that it will win are favorable. The theory fails to take into account the many adventurous wars which nations have begun against the odds. Moreover, power has never stayed in balance for long. To correct imbalance on the Continent, Britain has waged many coalition wars against the European nation strongest at the time. War as the classic method to correct imbalance hardly recommends the balance of power as a means for keeping the peace.

For that purpose, the balance of power sounds sensible but never has worked for long. If it had, would the history of nations have been a record of sanguinary wars? If it be answered that wars have resulted from imbalance, the short reply is: Then the balance must be inherently unstable.

From the beginning of history wars in Europe were chronic, but 1815 to World War I was peaceful by comparison. Perforce, proponents of the balance theory rely on that interlude which coincided with the so-called Pax Britannica. Both the period and Britain during it therefore deserve close scrutiny.

Long coalition wars often have been followed by a comparatively peaceful interlude because the participants have been exhausted, a condition that was especially severe after the more than 20 years of Europe's wars against revolutionary and Napoleonic France. From the end of these wars in 1815 to 1850 the fear of revolution pervaded the Courts of the Continental monarchs. Those fears and exhaustion contributed much to external peace.

The 1815-1850 peace on the Continent was not undisturbed. In addition to many bloody internal clashes, there were external wars. This period culminated with a bang in the 1848 wave of rebellions. They brought fighting in Germany, Austria, Sicily, and Italy and war between Austria and North Italy (Sardinia). Moreover, it was not the balance of power which caused this period on the Continent to be comparatively peaceful. From 1648 to 1815, there had been successive opposing coalitions and incessant wars between them. The striking fact about the 1815-1850 years was the complete absence of balancing coalitions.

From 1851 to 1878 Europe returned to normal. Wars on the Continent occurred in 1853, 1854-1856, 1859, 1864, 1866, 1870-1871, 1876, and 1877. The Pax Britannica on the Continent from 1851 to 1878 was neither peaceful nor Britannic.

From 1878 to 1911 the Balkans were restless. Carol I of Rumania suppressed five popular uprisings; it took 140,000 of his troops to put down the agrarian revolt of 1907. But apart from the Balkans and the overthrow of the King of Portugal in favor of a republic, the Continent enjoyed 33 years of peace.

Italy's 1911-1912 war against Turkey broke the long lull. The Balkan Wars of 1912-1913 against Turkey — promoted by Russia — and Bulgaria's war against the other Balkan countries over division of the spoils again broke the peace, which was shattered the following year by World War I.

The success of the Continental balance to keep the peace rests on 33 years (1878-1910). In fact, the period of balance was much shorter. The Triple Alliance in force at the start of World War I began as an 1879 alliance between Germany and Austria-Hungary. Though Italy fought on the other side in World War I, it should be counted on the German side of the scale from 1882, when Italy joined Germany and Austria-Hungary to form the Triple Alliance. The French-Russian balancing coalition, however, did not come into existence until 1893. At best, therefore, the balance kept the peace from 1893 until 1911. During that period, moreover, England was not a member of the French-Russian coalition. England discussed a German alliance in the 1890s and did not settle its extensive overseas territorial disputes with France until 1904 or with Russia until 1907.

Britain formed an entente with France about 1904-1905; the process was gradual. After the balance became perfect by the British-French entente added to the French-Russian alliance against the Triple Alliance, only a few years elapsed before the balanced coalitions went to war in the slaughter of 1914-1918. That record is scarcely favorable for the balance of power as a preserver of peace in Europe. It is easy to blame the statesmen of the fatal year 1914, but such personal fault finding fails to explain why wars have happened regularly through the ages.

In the rest of the world the Pax Britannica (1815-1913) was not British, and even more certainly it was not peaceful. The United States marched to the Pacific over the Indians and Mexicans, engaged in a bloody Civil War, and fought Spain. Japan did not emerge from its long period of nonintercourse with the rest of the world until the late 1860s but thereafter joined the fray. Japan defeated China in 1894; Russia in 1904-1905. Japan assumed a protectorate over Korea in 1907. Russia fought a long series of wars in Central Asia and expanded across Siberia to the Pacific. Weak China still waged wars against the great powers — with England (1839-1842) and with France and England (1856-1858). Foreigners helped suppress the Chinese T'ai Ping rebellion (1848-1865), and the Boxer rebellion of 1899-1901 developed into a war of China against the European powers. The French conquest of Algeria began in 1830; of Indochina in 1858. During the "century of peace," France fought much in Africa and Asia, not to mention Mexico. And the list in this paragraph is not complete.

For Britain the Pax Britannica was a century of overseas wars. At the outset of the period in protection of England's lucrative trade with Spanish America, British "volunteers," with connivance by the British government, aided in freeing South America from Spain. From 1837 through 1901 the luster of British arms did not tarnish; there was not a single year in which English soldiers did not fight on continents other than Europe.

1815-1913 was neither an era of peace nor a real exception. The regular wars on the Continent merely found another habitat and mostly were waged against weaker foes.

Closely akin to the balance of power theory is the idea of dividing the world into spheres of influence and assigning one to each great power or groups of powers. The spheres school of thought has considered the small nations as children upon whom quiet demeanor must be forced when they become a nuisance. This is more easily said than done. Moreover, spheres of influence presuppose a unity of purpose among the great powers that has never existed.

At Tilsit in 1807, the division of Europe into spheres of influence by Napoleon I and Tsar Alexander I of Russia ended in war between them five years later; meanwhile each had encroached on the other's sphere. World War I started in the Balkans, where the spheres of influence of Austria-Hungary (later joined by Germany) on the one hand, and Russia on the other, could not be kept constant. This was partly because one or the other of the great powers regularly sought an increased sphere and partly because the Balkan nations and factions within them all pursued their own advantages.

Since 1976 Henry Kissinger has been disappointed by the Soviet and Cuban incursions into Africa after Kissinger's 1972 détente with the USSR. Kissinger considered Africa at least a neutral sphere.

1890-1913 has been called the age of innocence, during which thinkers in western Europe and the United States tended to ignore the dark side of the nature of nations which the founding fathers had so clearly perceived. Woodrow Wilson, born in 1856, was led by the optimism of his era to put his faith in the Covenant of the League of Nations — a treaty — as his chosen instrument to keep the peace. As a 1920 vice-presidential candidate, Franklin D. Roosevelt, born in 1882, campaigned for the League, which he resurrected during World War II as the United Nations to keep the peace. For that purpose neither organization has been effectual. The Covenant of the League of Nations was tattered by breach and collapsed. The United Nations Charter has been broken regularly.

Our statesmen have constructed other policies for our peace and survival. Since 1947 the United States has pursued containment of communism, fathered by Kennan, though in his later years he has almost disowned his child. Whatever may be said for or against containment as a policy for our survival, containment has not been an instrument of peace. In following the policy we fought the North Koreans, the Chinese, the Viet Cong, and the North Vietnamese.

In 1972 Nixon and Kissinger superimposed détente on containment as an American peace policy. They did not abandon containment. In his 1974 brilliant defense of détente, Kissinger said: "We and the Soviets are bound to compete for the foreseeable future."[2] He further stressed that the competition would be military and political. If the volume of his words obscured the point, his actions removed any doubt. Kissinger upheld all our global alliances, and Nixon did not withdraw our troops from Europe, Japan, or Korea. Though the "settlement" with North Vietnam pulled the rug from under the South Vietnamese, Kissinger tried to supply them until Congress thwarted him, as he should have foreseen that Congress would under the lulling influence of détente. Kissinger believed that Salvador Allende Gossens (overthrown 1973) was bent on establishing a communist

2. H. A. Kissinger, statement presented to the Senate Committee on Foreign Relations, September 19, 1974, text, Department of State *Bulletin*, October 14, 1974, v. 71, No. 1842, pp. 505-519. The quotation is at p. 507.

regime in Chile; by subversive aid to Chilean dissidents Kissinger helped in preventing that outcome. In Angola Congress blocked Kissinger from further efforts to contest a communist seizure.

George Meany, President of the American Federation of Labor and Congress of Industrial Organizations, asked two pertinent questions: "What is the difference between détente and cold war? Isn't cold war also an avoidance of hot war?"[3] As Leonid Brezhnev has reiterated, the USSR has not abandoned the ideological struggle abroad. Moreover, American troops confront soldiers of the communist-ruled states in Europe and Asia. True, we have abandoned some of the outposts, but we still man what we consider to be the essential ramparts. The so-called cold war, of which proponents of détente speak in the past tense, was never cold, was not a war, and is not over.

To containment, détente added a policy of atmosphere: Don't treat the communist masters as ogres; be pleasant to them. Give them incentives for peace and to restrain their adventures abroad by trade concessions, cultural relations, and transfer of our technology. And of course make treaties with them, especially for arms control. In essence this is what Kissinger said in 1974.

Usually a national policy has been based on assumptions, which frequently have become the policy's habiliments and trappings, which in turn have become dogmas. Détente's underlying assumptions announced by Kissinger have come to be accepted as instruments of peace.

The first dogma of détente is: Trade between nations is conducive to peace between them. No. 6 of *The Federalist* asked: "Has commerce hitherto done anything more than change the objects of war?" Alexander Hamilton found a negative answer by reviewing historical precedents from Athens to his own day. In the year before each of the two great wars of this century between Germany and Russia — 1913 and 1940 — German-Russian trade reached its highest points. In the colonial expansion of the European nations the trader frequently opened the door for the conquering soldiers. Trade between the USSR and China reached its peak shortly before the break in their relations. Just

3. G. Meany, in testimony before the Senate Foreign Relations Committee, October 1, 1974, *AFL-CIO Free Trade Union News,* October 1974, v. 29, No. 9, p. 2.

before World War I there was extensive trade among all the belligerents.

Ancient, medieval, and modern history broaden these examples into a general pattern: Neighboring nations have been both the most regular trading partners and the most regular opponents in war. As commerce has broadened over the globe, so has war. The upshot of historical experience is that trade between nations has not tended to promote either peace or war between them.

A single snip from the pruning shears of history sends the next assumption headlong into the rubbish heap. Cooperation in energy, science, technology, and health plus cultural exchanges are said by Kissinger and his followers to be conducive to peace, and hence necessary for détente. But neighbors have regularly exchanged their cultures, sciences, and technologies — France-England, France-Germany, for example — while wars between them became a habit.

The next dogma of détente is that consultation between representatives of opposing nations is the route to peace. Yet from 1500 on, when European diplomatic channels have functioned extensively and intensively, war has been chronic. Personal relations among European diplomats have been generally cordial; their drinking and dining together at meetings have been so routine as to be unworthy of comment — all of which has not prevented repeated European wars. Many European monarchs have been related by ties of blood; when World War I started, the tsar of Russia and the king of England were both cousins of the German kaiser. The final reminder that personal association and even consanguinity are no bars to bloody conflicts is our own civil war.

Kissinger also emphasized summit meetings as conducive to peace. American experience with such meetings — Woodrow Wilson's in Paris in 1919 and Franklin D. Roosevelt's in Yalta in 1945 — should ring bells of warning rather than peals of good tidings. But for summit meetings as the road to peace, it is enough to remember British Prime Minister Neville Chamberlain's visit to Hitler at Munich in 1938, followed by war in 1939.

If Henry Kissinger the diplomat believed that the hard-bitten Soviet and Chinese leaders could be swayed by blandishments, Henry Kissinger the historian knew better. Though his hero Prince Klemens von Metternich was often opposed politically to Napoleon I, their personal relations were pleasant. In 1810 Napoleon married Marie Louise, daughter of the Austrian Emperor whom Metternich served. The next year she bore her husband a son, the heir to the French throne. Two years later Metternich brought Austria into the final coalition war against Napoleon. Doctor Kissinger wrote:

> Because the parvenu from Corsica identified obligation with personal relations, he could not conceive that a father might make war on the husband of his daughter. Because the House of Habsburg had learned in its reign of five hundred years that history transcends the individual, it consulted only the considerations which might ensure its permanence.[4]

Though most of the statesman's other tools are interesting in their own right, few merit more than brief mention as instruments of peace. Charitable foreign aid may be passed; its purpose is not to gain an advantage for the donor. In contrast, subsidy, which we also include as foreign aid, seeks to purchase governmental action or abstention. Bribery, though it has been usually administered by diplomats, has been employed in connection with every implement. Rarely has either the subsidized government or the recipient of the bribe stayed bought. Moreover, both subsidy and bribery matter little for keeping the peace. The same may be said of economic pressure such as the Arabs exerted by their 1973 oil embargo and of international cartels to raise prices. Conceivably such pressures could cause war; certainly they are not tools of peace.

The history of influencing subversions, designed to sway governments rather than to overthrow them, is a record of intrigues, deceits, and callous betrayals, but that is not why the tool deserves small attention here. Nuclear war is the only war that can jeopardize our survival. Influencing subversions will

4. H. A. Kissinger, *A World Restored*, Grosset & Dunlap, New York, 1964, p. 45.

have slight effect in preventing or causing such a war. Decisive subversions are discussed in the last two chapters.

Diplomacy is a useful patching tool for the short run, and as such is not to be sneered at as an auxiliary instrument of peace. Temporary settlement treaties and alliances, if not relied upon — but the if is large — fall in the same category. But the limitations of both treaties and diplomacy recommend neither as prime tools of our survival or of peace. And the 34th Chapter of Genesis should prompt us to write upon the doorpost of our house and upon its gates: Remember the Hivites.

CHAPTER 5

SALT or the Sheathed Nuclear Sword

Every specific action proposed by preceding and subsequent chapters for our survival and peace will take some years to complete. Meanwhile we must depend on our nuclear sword as a deterrent. Instead of blunting it by strategic arms limitations talks (SALT) treaties, we should sharpen and strengthen it.

The recurrent controversy over this subject brings to mind two historic debates. The superb orations of Demosthenes warning his Athenian fellow citizens against the designs of Philip of Macedonia failed; Philip won hegemony over Greece. Despite the eloquence of Winston Churchill, he almost lost the battle of words in England until Adolf Hitler attacked Poland to start World War II. Each great speaker fell short of fully arousing his countrymen because during the acrimonious argument about the facts the standard of judgment became blurred. Similarly, we debate the fairness to us of specific provisions of SALT treaties at length but forget that any SALT pact is only as trustworthy as the two tools on which we rely in making it: treaties and intelligence.

Although our statesmen indignantly deny relying on Soviet treaties, their actions speak louder than their words. President Jimmy Carter and Secretary of Defense Harold Brown confronted the Soviet chemical warfare threat by proposing a treaty "banning" such weapons. There is no way to verify whether the Soviets would continue to manufacture chemical weapons despite such a treaty. Aided by Henry Kissinger, Presidents Richard Nixon and Gerald Ford persuaded the Senate to consent to the totally unverifiable biological (bacteriological) warfare treaty. Be-

77

cause the USSR has attack submarines designed to assualt our ballistic missile-firing submarines, we worry that the sea arm of our nuclear deterrent may be paralyzed if the USSR discovers techniques to locate our submarines. Both sides are working on such techniques. Leslie H. Gelb, former national security correspondent of *The New York Times* and director of The State Department Bureau of Political-Military Affairs (1977-1979), proposes that we meet the threat by additional arms control treaties. "More work," he says, "needs to be done urgently on such ideas as limiting the production of attack submarines that can hunt down ballistic missile-firing subs and establishing safe areas in the ocean where subs may not go."[1]

In the light of Gelb's former exalted position in the State Department and as a maker of opinion, this passage shows how deeply our foreign policy establishment has been infected by treaty reliance. His first proposal is a pact limiting attack submarines to a given number. That would restrict us, but we could not know whether the USSR had or had not built all the components of attack submarines ready to assemble. It is the second proposal, however, which demonstrates utter credulity. By treaty Gelb would draw described lines in the oceans through which attack submarines of either party would be prohibited from passing. Nobody would pay any attention to such a treaty ban during or on the eve of war, the only time the prohibition would be important. In World War I Germany disregarded its Belgian neutrality treaty. More recently none of the parties observed the 1962 treaty declaring Laos out of bounds.

Secretary of Defense Harold Brown, speaking for President Jimmy Carter, exposed their disease of treaty-reliance in 1978 when Brown reported to Congress that the Soviets had the capability of destroying our satellites and to counter the threat proposed that we negotiate a treaty banning such attacks. We have tried to do so. Again who would pay any attention to such a treaty in time of war?

If in breach of a SALT treaty the USSR secretly created and then suddenly deployed more nuclear arms than the treaty per-

1. L.H. Gelb, "A Glass Half Full," *Foreign Policy*, No. 36, Fall, 1979, p. 29.

mitted, American cancellation of the treaty would not repair the damage. If we were overmatched by the deployment, our injury might well be fatal because of the long time it would take us to equal the Soviet arsenal. But this is impossible, the proponents of SALT claim. Through our intelligence, particularly our "national technical means of verification," we know what the Soviets are doing.

Our statesmen who have vociferously condemned our intelligence arm not only for its abuses, but also for its incompetence, now laud its ability to detect SALT violations. If, after deciding to hazard all his worldly goods in a poker game with a cardsharp, John Doe announced that he was relying on a foolproof system to detect cheating, his friends would deem him a fool. When we play SALT treaties with the USSR for our lives and justify our conduct by our ability to catch Soviet cheating, we are — to be polite — unwise. And apart from the character of our opponent, the lamp of intelligence always has flickered and misled. The intelligence process has been almost as untrustworthy as treaties.

Intelligence is not a tool to shape events; it is a lamp to illuminate. Save for misinformation to lead the enemy astray (plants) and counterintelligence to protect our own secrets, the sole purpose of intelligence is to furnish knowledge as a basis for decision. The product of intelligence is appraised information (sometimes called finished intelligence) procured by a government (including its military branch) in affairs abroad (including military combat) during war or peace. The intelligence process includes collecting the information, assaying it, and the resultant political and military decisions.

Providing intelligence to our executive branch is the assigned task of our "intelligence community," which includes our Central Intelligence Agency (CIA), the National Security Agency (NSA), and several agencies of our Department of Defense, with the State Department also performing some intelligence functions. NSA is our department of scientific eavesdropping. It intercepts messages of foes, allies, and neutrals and maintains an American "black chamber" for translating messages in secret writing (codes or ciphers) into readable form.

Despite the billions we spend annually on intelligence, we

have been regularly surprised. President Carter complained that his intelligence arm misled him on Iran. He mistakenly assumed that this — as he thought — isolated failure was not typical and could be cured by an order to be more efficient. In fact, American intelligence frequently has erred, but not because its practitioners have been either numskulls or knaves. Had Carter studied the history of the tool, he would have discovered that the intelligence of all nations has been unreliable.

David Kahn devoted many years to his excellent study of Nazi intelligence, and he had complete access to all the records.[2] He found German intelligence incompetent, particularly at the top. Although Anglo-American intelligence was better than German, if Kahn had studied the intelligence of any nation with the same admirable thoroughness, he would have reached the same conclusion. Immediately preceding and during World War II, intelligence errors of the gravest sort occurred everywhere, were in the judging process, and mostly at the top.

To begin at home, we hardly covered ourselves with glory by being surprised at Pearl Harbor or later at the Battle of the Bulge. Britain and France disregarded the Nazi preparation for war. Britain failed to gather and take account of the information that was easiest to obtain: evidence of the weakness of its French ally. Though warned by the British, Joseph Stalin was surprised by the Nazi attack and lost hundreds of thousands of soldiers. There were no intelligence heroes at the top. This untrustworthiness will necessarily continue, because intelligence is a guessing game with each country trying to outwit and mislead its adversaries.

Our own intelligence estimates have missed the mark widely in vital matters. In 1941 we estimated that Germany would defeat Russia in three months. The same year we were surprised at Pearl Harbor. We were again surprised by the North Korean attack on South Korea, by China's attack against General Douglas MacArthur's forces when we invaded North Korea, by the 1956 Israeli-English-French attack on Egypt, and by the Arabs' 1973 Yom Kippur attack against Israel.

2. D. Kahn, *Hitler's Spies*, Macmillan, New York, 1978.

Our record in appraising Soviet nuclear strength is scarcely reassuring. In 1949 the Soviets exploded a fission (atom) bomb. Our intelligence community had estimated that it would take the USSR several more years to develop one. Four years later the Soviets had a fusion (hydrogen) bomb. Again we misgauged the time factor; the USSR acquired the hydrogen bomb faster than we judged it would. The USSR's 1957 Sputnik and its development of an intercontinental ballistic missile (ICBM) surprised us completely. In the "missile gap" controversy, which John F. Kennedy exploited in the 1960 presidential campaign, we overestimated Soviet ICBMs. At the same time, we greatly underestimated the number of intermediate and medium-range ballistic missile launchers that the USSR would deploy at the end of the 1950s and in the early 1960s. The two errors roughly canceled each other. In judging whether American intelligence has been trustworthy, it is immaterial that we made one overestimate equalized by one underestimate. The significant point is that both our appraisals were incorrect.

Ever since, our intelligence community has been underestimating total expected Soviet nuclear strength. In 1974 Professor Albert Wohlstetter of the University of Chicago analyzed public data to test the accuracy of our estimates.[3] His was no comparison of apples with oranges; Wohlstetter used a Defense Department report that estimated future Soviet nuclear deployment and matched it with a subsequent Defense Department report which recorded the deployment after it had occurred. In every case we had grossly underestimated.

We have also greatly underrated Soviet military spending, which weighs heavily on the scale for gauging Soviet nuclear capacity. In 1976 our Defense Department admitted that from 1969 on it had stated total Soviet military expenditures as half of Soviet actual military spending. A miss by half for eight years was a miss indeed.

Our intelligence process has proved unworthy of trust. And since 1972 we have fallen under the spell cast upon us by the

3. A. Wohlstetter, *Legends of the Strategic Arms Race*, United States Strategic Institute, Report 75-1, Washington, 1975.

wonders of scientific surveillance and have come to believe that we know "facts" about Soviet nuclear strength which we do not and cannot know.

Until 1972 we refused to make arms control treaties that did not provide for on-site inspections to verify performance. This long-held American position succumbed in the 1972 SALT treaties to "national technical means of verification," the words used in the pacts as a euphemism for scientific surveillance. The technical means are principally our eyes in the sky — satellites and aircraft overflying enemy land and photographing it — aided by various electronic and other detection instruments. But our supposedly all-seeing eyes in the sky, supported by every technical device we have, do not and cannot give us the information we need about Soviet nuclear strength.

We can count deployed bombers, other aircraft, surface ships, submarines, and the number of tubes they have for launching. We cannot determine, however, whether Soviet submarines contain additional submarine-launched ballistic missiles (SLBMs). We have tailored both the SALT I Interim Agreement and the SALT II Agreement to our ability to count rather than to our need to know. Neither pact limits the number of nuclear *missiles;* each limits the number of nuclear *launchers,* and it is with the number of launchers that Defense Department reports deal. Nonetheless, these reports are generally treated as a comparison of Soviet and American nuclear strength in *missiles.*

We can count land silos that house launchers, but we cannot know whether additional ICBMs are stored nearby or elsewhere. Among Soviet ICBMs, at least the SS-17s and the giant SS-18s employ a cold launch, in which the rocket motors do not ignite until the missiles are clear of their silos. Hence, the missiles do not burn up their launchers as our missiles do in their "hot" launch. At long last, Secretary of Defense Harold Brown has admitted the refire capability of the SS-17 and SS-18 and that the Soviets have excess missiles.[4]

In 1977 Major General George Keegan, who in January of that year had retired from his post as Chief of Air Force Intelligence, related how the USSR acquired its cold-launch technique,

4. *Annual Defense Department Report FY 1981,* p. 80.

the failure of our intelligence to take it into account, and the resultant large Soviet superiority. The Soviets picked up "a Boeing design [which] we didn't want," and which *Aviation Week & Space Technology* published. The Soviets improved it. Keegan estimated in 1977 that the USSR had between 500 and 3,000 additional ICBMs that could be fired from Soviet launchers with a refire capacity. When it is remembered that in 1980 the United States has only 1,054 ICBMs, the seriousness of Keegan's claim can be appreciated. Moreover, it is unnecessary to accept his statement about numbers. We can arrive at the same point by deduction: it beggars reason to assume that the Soviets would develop a refire capability and manufacture no missiles to refire.

Our eyes in the sky cannot look into caves, mines, or structures in which missiles can be hidden. There are endless ways of concealing nuclear offensive missiles, and the same is true of some elements of antiballistic- missile (ABM) installations.

If we cannot count missiles, obviously we cannot count warheads, but we suffer from a further inability. The number of warheads the USSR has depends on how many of its missiles are armed with multiple independent re-entry vehicles (MIRVs) and the number of MIRVs per missile. The report of the 1976 Senate Select Committee investigating our military intelligence stated that detecting "MIRV missiles which are concealed in silos or submarines" would be highly difficult.[5]

While we know that the USSR has cruise missiles, we cannot determine their number or their range. And even an expert looking at a cruise missile cannot tell whether it is conventional or nuclear.

Once it is realized that we cannot count enemy missiles, warheads, or cruise missiles, the very basis of our technical means of verification collapses. The future of verification is even gloomier. Since Hiroshima, atomic/nuclear weapons have improved not only in size, destructiveness, and range, but also in quality. The quality trend is the prominent one now, and it seems likely to continue. Quality is impossible to verify.

5. Report No. 94-755, 94th Congress, 2nd Session, Senate, *Foreign and Military Intelligence*, Book 1, U.S. Government Printing Office, Washington, 1976, p. 322.

National technical means of verification are indeed marvelous, but they do not enable us to estimate Soviet nuclear strength reliably. The refinement in the quality of nuclear weapons that may be expected augurs a decrease in our abilty to measure.

Our mistakes have occurred during our possession of scientific intelligence as well as before. For example, in the middle 1970s we underestimated the size and efficacy of the USSR'S MIRV program and the time required for attainment of increased accuracy for their MIRVs. Nor have our errors ceased. A comparison of the charts in our Defense Department reports for fiscal years 1979 and 1980 shows our underestimation in 1978. The fiscal year 1981 report concedes a previous gross underestimation of North Korean forces.[6]

The trouble with intelligence goes deeper than our own failures and inadequacies. The inherent defect of intelligence as an instrument on which to base survival lies partly in the fuels that feed the lamp. Human spies have often been inaccurate or double agents. Long ago Niccolò Machiavelli pointed out the folly of believing refugees. Cryptology is a wonderful art, but planting misinformation in radio messages is easy. And so-called scientific intelligence is also subject to planted misinformation.

It is not only obtaining the raw information that causes errors; grave mistakes have occurred and will recur in appraisal of the information by competent military and civilian officials. Before the Yom Kippur War, the Israeli intelligence service was rated as among the best in the world — some rated it as the best — yet the Egyptian-Syrian attack achieved surprise on October 6, 1973, with the unmobilized Israeli reserves in the synagogues. After the war, the Israeli Agranat Inquiry Commission found that its army intelligence possessed a vast amount of information indicating an attack. The error was in appraisal.

The more certain and seemingly scientific the information, the greater is the likelihood of being deceived by over-reliance. During World War II the excellent German cipher machine was called Enigma, to solve which the British constructed a machine named the Bomb. By many radio intercepts of German ciphered messages and cryptanalysis of them, the British and Americans

6. *Annual Defense Department Report FY 1981*, p. 50.

were reading the enemy's mail. The product was called Ultra — a deserved name — and was furnished to commanders in the field. General Erwin Rommel surprised and defeated the Americans at Kassarine Pass in North Africa. Before the attack, Rommel had enforced complete radio silence. General Dwight D. Eisenhower's chief of intelligence had come to depend on Ultra and assumed from the absence of Ultra information that there would be no attack.

Time passed, and Eisenhower was again surprised because of overreliance on Ultra. When Adolf Hitler was planning his December 1944 Ardennes offensive, he directed that no orders concerning the attack be sent by radio. From aerial reconnaissance, prisoner of war interrogation, and old-fashioned order of battle intelligence, the information that poured into American headquarters, both Eisenhower's and Omar Bradley's, ordinarily would have led to the belief that a German attack was imminent, but no preparations to meet it were made. Near castastrophe resulted when the Germans obtained complete surprise. They might have split the American and British forces save for fortuitous circumstances and heroic fighting by the Americans and British. The American commanders did not act on their abundant information because they had come to lean too heavily on Ultra as their primary source. When Ultra dried up, Eisenhower and Bradley assumed there would be no attack. This was not a case of the enemy's misleading by a plant; it was a case of self-deception. The absence of Ultra was given precedence over other positive information.

Assaying is somewhat easier during peace than in the heat of battle. But when the United States was at peace in 1941, General George C. Marshall, Admiral H. R. Stark, and President Roosevelt made an appraisal error based on cryptanalysis and self-deception just as Eisenhower and Bradley did three years later. The American Basic Navy War Plan of May 26, 1941, explicity envisioned the probability of a surprise Japanese attack on our fleet at Pearl Harbor, but after August the danger seemed to have slipped from the minds of all the responsible officers and their civilian superiors. Pearl Harbor was a typical instance of apparently foolproof secret data that led to a wrong assay. It was not the hand being quicker than the eye, but the attraction of the eye away from the target guided by the bright light of sure secret information. We had broken the Japanese code and were intercepting the abundant Japanese radio messages. They were silent about Pearl Harbor but in October-November 1941 were directing a movement south toward the Malay Peninsula, which led us to overlook the likelihood of an attack on Pearl Harbor. Those who understood the worth of capabilities neglected them because they believed that they knew all.

While such self-deception or a plant is easier by scientific means than in human spying because of the aura of seeming certainty which hovers over science, assaying is difficult no matter what type of information fuels the lamp. The appraisal of raw information is the judging process that takes place in the courtroom, in battle, and in affairs abroad during peace. As the CIA has justly stressed, the assessment of the information is equally as important as its gathering. The weighing is not easy. Facts do not march in review before the appraiser bearing labelled placards, frequently the evidence is in conflict, and all the information must be jelled into a pattern upon which a judgment can be based.

Intelligence in our time has one other serious defect: the tremendous volume of information. Add together all the radio messages our National Security Agency (NSA) intercepts, the reports from human sources, the daily photographs taken by our eyes in the sky, the technical data, the influx from our embassies, the public information, and the analyses. The sum is a sea of paper in which our intelligence chiefs must flounder.

In September 1979 the State Department said that our intelligence arm during both the Gerald Ford and Jimmy Carter administrations had sufficient photographic information to identify a Soviet brigade in Cuba but failed to examine and analyze the photographs. The claim — true or false — emphasizes that we are drowning in our volume of information. No intelligence chief, much less the President, can find time to read all of it, let alone to understand it well enough to use it in timely decisions.

We tend to think in terms of abstractions. If instead of "intelligence," we contemplate the many thousand human beings who collect and analyze the information on which our finished intelligence estimates are based, and if we then consider the human weaknesses of our intelligence personnel in terms of the people we deal with every day, we will bring intelligence down to the level it deserves.

If treaties and intelligence are untrustworthy, then SALT treaties based on them must be undependable. The most apt modern example of the failure of a disarmament treaty combines a breach of the treaty, the deficiency of on-site inspections, and a breakdown in detection through intelligence. Though the Soviet Union was not a party to the treaty, it aided and abetted the violations. In the peace treaty closing World War I, Germany gave the victorious Allies clear detailed promises not to rearm. Not content with a paper chain without provisions for verification, the Allies established in the 1919 Treaty of Versailles the most thorough and comprehensive system of on-site inspections ever devised. The Allied Control Commission stationed in Germany was given unlimited access to every installation in the country, every day, at any time.

Many remember that Hitler tore up the treaty; few recollect what happened before Hitler. The German republic began to rearm in violation of the treaty from the day it was made. German rearmament progressed well even while the Control Commission was stationed in Germany. In the spirit of Locarno — the détente of the 1920s — the commission was withdrawn in 1927; the German republic intensified the rearmament. From the beginning the Soviets actively assisted the Germans in these violations. From 1921 to 1933 the USSR and the German republic concluded a series of secret military agreements for the USSR to manufacture poison gas, airplanes, motors, and the like for Germany and for the delivery of other Soviet munitions to Germany. In return the Germans trained Soviet pilots, instructors, and technical experts.

The statesman tends to trust his intelligence lamp because sometimes it shines brightly and steadily. When it flickers, he summons his repairmen to fix it. There always has been, however, an unfixable defect in the intelligence lamps of all countries, whether antique models or the latest creation. A maxim about intelligence need contain only nine words: "We don't know, we can't know, remember Pearl Harbor."

Perhaps the greatest sin of the SALT process is that it has perpetuated and codified by the ABM treaty our lack of nuclear defense. Though the ABM treaty has a six-months cancellation clause, we are not likely to exercise it until we understand the defects of SALT.

Since the SALT I treaties, we have lost ground because the Soviets have heavily outspent us. The negotiations and the uncertainty of their outcome have slowed our arms development in fields not covered by the treaties because since SALT we have regarded new weapons as bargaining chips. For example, in 1976 the Defense Department told Congress:

> Both the ALCM [air launched cruise missile] and SLCM [sea launched cruise missile] are an important issue in the ongoing SALT II negotiations. Pending outcome of these negotiations, we are preceeding with the two programs at a deliberate pace during the advanced development phase, when expenditures are relatively low compared to the engineering developing phase; this will allow us to accomodate SALT developments and still maintain an orderly development effort.[7]

We slackened the speed of our development of the cruise missile because we did not want to spend too much on a missile which might be banned by the next treaty.

Because draftsmen are unable to think of all the cases that may arise, and because technology soon makes SALT treaties obsolete, the treaties cannot perform their purported tasks of arms control. We left large holes in the Space and SALT I treaties, which the Soviets walked through, just as the Japanese did in the naval treaties of the 1920s and 1930s.

The chief argument for SALT treaties is their preservation of peace. SALT treaties do not settle or ameliorate the causes of deep hostility between the USSR and the United States; the pacts are not even a patch on the determination of the Soviet Union to impose communist rule. The 1935 British-Nazi naval limitation treaty, which Hitler broke, did nothing to stop him;

7. *Annual Defense Department Report FY1977*, p. 88.

thereafter he became more aggressive. Since 1972 the Soviets have become more adventurous. There are only two effective methods of preventing war: avoidance and deterrence. SALT treaties do not affect avoidance; since 1972 our deterrent has weakened.

It is almost impossible to negotiate a SALT treaty fair to us. We started wrong when we conceded too much in the 1972 Interim Agreement. There are inherent disadvantages to us in any arms limitations talks with the Soviets. Theirs is a closed society; ours is an open one; hence they always will know more about our weapons than we know about theirs. On the Soviet leaders there are no internal pressures to reach argreement: ours have the temptation to announce a triumph of peace to help their domestic political fortunes.

As these lines are written, the Senate has not yet given its consent to the SALT II Agreement. This chapter has deliberately avoided the debate about whether in truth we have rough equivalence and about the terms of particular SALT treaties, including the SALT II Agreement, because if we choose a proper standard of judgment, the opposing claims will resolve themselves. Nonetheless, the assertion by many distinguished experts that in 1980-1981 we probably will become inferior to the USSR in nuclear weapons and that we will be in grave peril for six or seven years should give us pause. The very existence of the debate proves that we need a stronger nuclear sword. Our representatives have no right to gamble with our safety.

Let it be granted, nevertheless, for the sake of the argument, that we have rough equivalence. Rough equivalence is rough but not equivalence. The vast land area of the USSR as compared to the United States puts us at an inherent disadvantage. Our population is more concentrated; the 1,000 Soviet cities we have to hit compared to our 140 cities the Soviets have to hit is another inferiority for us. Soviet civil defense is a third. To be sure, we can equal it, but that will take time. Finally, there is the first strike which we have forsworn. Equivalance is not equivalence when one side has the sole choice of the time for nuclear war. True, we could strike first, as the Soviets would be quick to reply, but we know we will not. It is likely therefore that any future SALT agreement will be unfair to us.

Even if rejection of SALT would require us to expend a huge additional amount for nuclear deterrence, that is no argument for SALT. There is a difference in kind between our primary objective of survival as a free people and our secondary objective of "the general welfare" or prosperity. A dead American scarcely can enjoy his welfare. But the whole idea of our being impoverished by the cost of nuclear weapons is a fantasy. For fiscal year 1981 our programmed outlays for nuclear weapons and their manning, including an allocation of overhead, amounted to less than 3 percent of the federal budget.

The cruise missile is comparatively inexpensive. Although whether it has been overrated remains to be seen, the cruise missile is important as a symbol of other weapons to come. In the long run we are more likely to save money without SALT treaties than with them. If we give our science and technology free rein, over the long pull probably we will develop simpler and cheaper weapons.

The period of American nuclear strength was from World War II until Lyndon Johnson began SALT negotiations, which continued under Richard Nixon, Ford, and Carter. During the administrations of Johnson, Nixon, Ford, and Carter American nuclear strength has waned while that of the USSR has waxed.

Some have doubted our willingness to spend the money required for deterrence and defense. Our would-be protectors against ourselves underrate the good sense of the American people, who are not heedless of their safety. SALT treaties have been popular because they have been dressed in the garments of peace and survival. But if the doomsayers about our will are right, we shall succumb in any event, and no treaty will save us.

The statement that there is no alternative to SALT treaties makes the false assumption that they are a requisite of nuclear peace. The alternative is to abandon SALT and sharpen and strengthen our nuclear sword. Ever since we started SALT our deterrent has weakened. If we strive for superiority, even if we do not achieve it, we shall probably attain at least true equivalence in the trying.

Hawks seldom voice the chief reason for additional American nuclear strength. Correctly, they talk about the danger of

Soviet political blackmail, but that is not the principal reason for a stronger American nuclear sword. The main reason is our survival and peace in the nuclear age.

The final supposed instrument for our salvation in the nuclear age is the clerical and lay preaching of peace. For the good intentions of such heralds, God bless them; from our being guided by their advice, God save us.

For the benefit of humankind, peace foundations advocate disarmament. They total the amount spent for weapons and show how much human misery could be relieved if the sum were diverted to that purpose. True, but as James Madison answered in *The Federalist* (No. 41):

> With what color of propriety could the force necessary for defense be limited by those who cannot limit the force of offense?... The means of security can only be regulated by the means and danger of attack.... If one nation maintains constantly a disciplined army,... it obliges the most pacific nations within the reach of its enterprises to take corresponding precautions.

George Washington's advice in his Farewell Address still holds true: The best assurance for peace is to be well prepared for war.

To rebut that proposition, antimilitarists contend that a large military establishment causes war. They argue that if a country creates strong armed forces, rulers will be unable to resist the temptation to use them to gain fame. But when the causes of aggression are scrutinized, blaming armed might for war is putting the cart before the horse. The incessant wars of Louis XIV of France were not waged because he had a fine standing army; he brought the army into being because he had an unquenchable thirst for glory. The existence of armies has not created the wars; rulers have created the armies that have fought the wars as instruments of the purposes of the rulers.

Still, it cannot be denied that all extensive conquerors have been well armed. Philip II of Macedonia (382-336 B. C.) created the army with which his son Alexander the Great aspired to conquer the world. And on his accession in 1740 Frederick the Great quickly employed for aggression against Austria the fine Prussian army he inherited from his father.

Nor can it be doubted that weak armed might has invited attack. From 1672 to 1678 Louis XIV fought Holland, Spain, the Habsburg Austrian Emperor, Denmark, Brandenburg, and a number of other German states. After the 1678-1679 peace treaties with his opponents, Louis kept his army on a war footing, while his adversaries demobilized. From 1679 to 1684, either by a show of force or by military assault, Louis annexed large territories, including Strassbourg, the rest of Alsace, Luxemburg, and cities in the Spanish Netherlands. Similarly, Britain's pacifism and disarmament after World War I encouraged Adolf Hitler to start World War II.

Examples can be multiplied on each side. The upshot of history is: Often nations that were prepared for war have waged offensive war; often nations that were unprepared have been subjected to attack.

Strong armed might will not insure us against attack but will tend to deter an assault and protect us against it if we add shelter and shield. This is the best we can do because there is no way to keep nations from arming. Even if all nations were to disarm, what is to stop one or more from rearming? The chance that our strong armed might could result in an American war of conquest is worth taking when considered against the alternative — the risk of being conquered or destroyed because we are not well armed.

Of the necessity for our military establishment there can be no doubt. The tool that takes precedence over all others is armed might, for only under its aegis can the statesman wield his other tools. To an antimilitarist it is axiomatic that military expenditures are wasteful. They would be in an ideal world, as would be policemen and locks on doors. In the real world, those who count a dollar spent for arms as a dollar lost to the social services forget that the indispensable service our government must do for us is to keep us alive and free. The best tool of peace is strong armed might.

* * * * *

For our survival and peace in the nuclear age, what should we do? Realize that whatever we do, nuclear war is likely sooner or later. Prepare the best shelter (civil defense) for our population that money and brains can buy. Go all out to develop an active defense. Know that treaties are a trap and avoid them except in the case of temporary settlement treaties and alliance treaties, and understand that they too will be broken. Comprehend that diplomacy is only a patching tool; use it for that purpose, though sparingly, but do not harbor the illusion that diplomacy can do more than patch. Forget SALT. Build up our nuclear deterrent to strive for superiority. In short, employ armed might in being as our tool of choice for survival and peace.

Nuclear war, however, is not inevitable. We should devote our utmost endeavor to prevent it by avoidance as well as deterrence. The next chapter is about that subject.

CHAPTER 6

The Unlearned Lesson of Vietnam

Even a mediocre statesman would have no difficulty in leading a nation of heroes, but such nations exist only in dreams. In the real world, if leaders overload the fortitude of their people, any nation will falter. Our leaders have not learned this core lesson of Vietnam; for they continue to place upon the shoulders of the American people onerous and unfair foreign burdens.

No one of our numerous Vietnamese blunders was the cause of the collapse of our home front; it caved in from the totality and cumulative effect. We were unwilling to go on because our leaders had imposed on us burdens too heavy to bear, not in loss of life or property, but in upheaval at home. This was not because we were Americans but because we were human. Vietnam's core message is the frailty of humankind.

A people will endure more during war than in peace. The facing off as antagonists between the USSR and the United States — whether called the cold war or not — has lasted much longer than any hot war in our history and is likely to continue for a long time unless ended by another hot war.

Ever since the cold war began, many commentators have characterized its essence as a struggle for the hearts and minds of people or as a battle of wills and have highlighted the American people as the leader of the free world in the conflict between opposing social systems. The gist of such comment may be put: The home front is the most important, and on it fortitude is the main thing. But though commentators have voiced this substance in one manner of expression or another, they have been less successful in finding how to cultivate fortitude, a virture hard to come by and even harder to keep. To be David, the brave hero of the moment, is far easier than to be Job, who held his faith through his grievous long continued afflictions. There are few Jobs.

In common with most other people, we American are prone to fancy ourselves to be somewhat better than the rest of mankind. But Winston Churchill was right in finding it difficult to believe that the European emigrants, who brought to our new land the virtues of the old countries from which they sprang, left behind all their vices.[1] Like all other people, we Americans have our weaknesses. If our leaders ask too much of us, our response will falter. The essence of statesmanship in sustaining the fortitude of the American people is for our leaders not to overburden it.

They have in our relations with our allies. Our presidents have proclaimed that we will make any sacrifice and bear any burden for defense of the free world. As a condition, however, they have not required our allies to make equal sacrifices or to bear commensurate burdens.

The founding fathers would have found our alliance with Japan hard to reconcile with our supposed Yankee shrewdness. The Japanese are an able, industrious, and disciplined people. These admirable qualities account in part for the Japanese commercial and industrial success since World War II, but far from wholly. One reason Japan has become rich is because the United States has paid the price of Japanese defense.

Our defense treaty with Japan is one-sided. Japan does not guard us and has nothing to guard us with. The financial disparity is both current and cumulative. Currently the Japanese bear only some part of the cost of American troops stationed in Japan for its defense. For many years, however, we paid the entire expense.

Our military expenditures have shrunk to about 5 percent of our gross national product (GNP), but during most of the years of our Japanese alliance, the percentage has been much higher. In contrast, the Japanese defense budget has been steadily less than 1 percent of Japanese GNP, and still is.

The inequality of our alliance is also in peril. In any war

1. W. S. Churchill, *The Aftermath 1918-1928*, Scribner's, New York, 1929, p. 129.

started by the USSR it would try to disable an adversary capable of delivering nuclear missiles or bombs on the Soviet homeland. Hence, a potential opponent of the USSR increases its danger by possessing a nuclear arsenal. The Japanese do not permit American nuclear arms on Japanese soil. The Japanese position is: Let the United States protect Japan at American jeopardy; let the United States, but not Japan, be a nuclear target.

Japan has ample manpower and wealth to defend itself, but its experience in World War II converted it to pacifism. This is a choice for Japan. The Japanese choice, however, becomes our concern when Japanese pacifism is translated into American defense of Japan.

Because of geographic position, the Japanese consider South Korea in unfriendly hands as a dagger pointed at their heart. If North Korea conquered South Korea, the dagger would not be pointed at us; it would be pointed, if at all, at Japan. Yet for over a quarter of a century we have been bearing part of the cost of Korean defense, and we continue to pay our troops stationed in Korea. Granted that South Korea needs arms to match the North Koreans, it speaks volumes about our attitude that we have not demanded that Japan pay the share we bear of the cost. We have not even dared mention that Japan should help.

South Korea may need a year to train replacements for American soldiers and airmen, but with a population approximately two and a fifth times that of North Korea, South Korea needs no Americans for its defense. Yet President Jimmy Carter's plan to withdraw American ground forces over a period of five years met with roars of disapproval from American hawks, and Carter still proposed leaving American airmen in South Korea.

The founding fathers would not have tolerated the sharing of burdens between us and our European allies. Of the total military spending by all the countries in the North Atlantic Treaty Organization (NATO), the United States contributed 75 percent in 1955, 73 percent in 1960, 70 percent in 1965, 71 percent in 1970, and 70 percent in 1975. The proportion was still 60 percent in 1978. Except for Greece and Turkey, where our aid has supplied a large part of their military expenditures, each of our other NATO allies spends for defense far less proportionately of its GNP than we do.[2] Per capita, Americans pay much more for defense than do Europeans in any of the NATO countries.[3] And when grants in aid and cumulative spending are considered, the disproportion is greater, and it still continues.

Excluding Greece and Turkey, our European NATO allies have a larger population than the USSR. The European NATO nations almost equal the Warsaw Pact nations in population and far exceed them in GNP and capital. In 1978 Secretary of Defense Harold Brown said: "We are fortunate in having prosperous and willing allies."[4] Prosperous they are; willing they have not been.

Prosperous West Germany is the front line country being defended. Yet even the West German offsetting of our balance of payments deficit, which did not alter the real disparity in outlay, was cancelled with our consent in 1976. The West Germans'

2. International Peace Research Institute, *Bulletin of Peace Proposals*, No. 3, Oslo, 1976, p. 252; Stockholm International Peace Research Institute, *Yearbook 1976*, pp. 123-144. The figures of both peace organizations on cost of armaments are widely respected. For 1978 and for comparison of percentages of GNPs see *Annual Department of Defense Report FY1981*, p. 221.

3. *U. S. News & World Report*, May 16, 1977, v. 82 No. 19, pp. 20-21, source International Institute for Strategic Studies, London. The French journal *Défense Nationale*, January 1977 stated the current percentages of defense spending in relation to GNP as: Belgium, 3; Canada, 2; Denmark, 2.6; France, 3.9; West Germany, 3.6; Greece, 6.5; The Netherlands, 3.6; Norway, 3.2; Britain, 5.1; Italy, 2.8; the United States, 6.1. *Aviation Week & Space Technology*, March 21, 1977, p. 41, listed defense expenditures of NATO countries in current prices in local currency. Using International Monetary Fund, *International Financial Statistics for GNPs*, Washington, January 1977, the figures translate into defense expenditures in relation to GNP as follows:

	1971	1972	1973	1974	1975	1976
France	3.9	3.8	3.7	3.6	not available	
West Germany	3.3	3.4	3.4	3.6	3.6	3.5
Britain	4.9	5.1	4.8	5.1	5.0	5.1
United States	7.0	6.6	6.0	6.1	6.0	5.9

Annual Defense Department Report FY 1981, p. 221 says that on defense the United States spends about 5 percent of our GNP; our European allies average 3.5 percent. This calculation, however, includes Greece and Turkey, whose percentages are higher than those of our western European allies, and neglects our grants in aid.

4. *Annual Defense Department Report FY 1979*, p. 3.

"economic miracle" was in part the result of their free competition, hard work, brains, and discipline. It is equally true, however, that one reason West Germany became wealthy is because the American people have shouldered the major load of its defense.

Other positions taken by some of our European allies have been unfair to us. If the USSR overran West Germany, France would be in the direct line of Soviet advance. Nonetheless France has played games with NATO, including ejecting it from its country.

Neither Denmark nor Norway permits nuclear weapons on its soil. The Danes and Norwegians feel that it is all right for Americans to be a nuclear target but not them.

Assume for the sake of the argument that it is necessary to keep some American troops in Europe and Asia to reassure our allies that we will fight if they are attacked. In *The Guns of August*, Barbara Tuchman relates a 1910 conversation between the British General Henry H. Wilson and the French General Ferdinand Foch. When Wilson inquired about the smallest British military force in France that would help the French, Foch answered that a single British soldier would be enough. He added that the French would see to it that the soldier was killed.

No matter how small our force in West Germany is, it insures our involvement in war if the USSR attacks West Germany. We cannot justify keeping many soldiers in West Germany at American expense when the West Germans, and even more all our NATO allies, have both the manpower and the wealth to replace our troops.

Our leaders have laid other foreign loads on the shoulders of the American people. By 1795 we had shed our alliance with France, and except for Indian treaties, we did not make another alliance pact until 1942. It would have astonished the founding fathers to learn that their successors have promised to participate in the defense of over 40 nations. Though under none of our treaties do we unequivocally agree to go to war if one of these nations is attacked by a communist-ruled state, such is the spirit of the pacts, and they are so understood by the United States, our allies, and our adversaries.

Besides the legal and moral obligations we have assumed — and in good conscience we ought to take them seriously — we have scattered our military forces over the globe. To carry out our commitments, in fiscal year 1979 we stationed overseas approximately 516,000 military and 148,000 civilian personnel, not to mention their dependents. The numbers have not appreciably changed.

Our world military presence sometimes is justified by it stabilizing effect in maintaining the balance of power, which never has remained stable, and which only war has restored temporarily. In addition, our statesmen tell us that our global military dispositions are for the purpose of keeping peace. History does not sustain the thesis that a far-flung military presence prevents involvement of a nation in war. The Roman Empire was constantly fighting. In modern history, the most apt precedent is the British Empire from 1815 to World War I. On the Continent where there were no British troops or bases, Britain fought hardly at all. Overseas, where the British maintained troops and bases, England fought incessant wars.

American bases and men in Japan and the Philippines failed to deter the Korean War. Despite our military presence in Taiwan, the Chinese bombarded Quemoy and Matsu and made one abortive attempt to take them. Although we could have delivered a naval and air assault on China from our bases in Japan and the Philippines, China conquered Tibet and attacked India.

We have become so accustomed to our far-flung dispositions that we do not realize their departure from our traditions. To the founding fathers and to their successors before the post-World War II period, stationing American troops all over the world during peace would have been an aberration. And once we place our men abroad we seem unable to remove them. But the greatest anomaly in our stance is this: Our military presence overseas in the name of peace is the worst possible posture for avoiding an American war.

After the Korean War, many senior American military officers warned us against fighting another conventional war on the Asiatic mainland. After Vietnam, they reiterated the warning.

In our wars in Korea and Vietnam we faced adversaries with practically no navy or air force. Nevertheless, we settled for a draw in Korea and lost in Vietnam. The vast reaches of the Pacific Ocean, the tremendous area of the mainland of Asia, and its numerous people all counsel against another such war.

Our Asian forces are too few to defend the noncommunist nations of Asia in a conventional war. Even if it be granted that our troops there are a deterrent, it is attained by their hostage character to insure our involvement in an Asian war that the American people are unwilling to fight. We are betting that our presence will deter a war at the price of being in one if the gamble fails.

To the founding fathers "the common defense" meant defense of the United States, and they contemplated no long-term alliances. Franklin D. Roosevelt believed it would be impossible to keep our troops in Europe on any but a temporary basis. Only since 1947 have we draped our defense mantle over all the sundry.

No one seduced us into assuming our present position; we maneuvered ourselves into it by a series of steps, some of which probably were justified when taken. In 1947, Britain, weakened by the losses of two world wars, could not help financially; France was in disarray. West Germany was in ruins and in any case not our ally. Greece seemed about to fall prey to a communist overthrow. The atom bomb was new; its delivery on target in distant places was a problem. Because there was no other country able to step into the defense gap, Harry Truman announced our financial aid to Greece and Turkey, subsequently broadened to the Truman Doctrine, and in 1949 extended to the North Atlantic Treaty. Our peacetime overseas presence commenced.

We started cautiously. In recommending the consent of the Senate to the North Atlantic Treaty in June 1949, the Senate Foreign Relations Committee said: "The committee emphasizes that this clearly does not commit any of the parties to declare war."[5] Since then successive presidents have declared that if our allies are attacked, we will fight. We have taken that decision

5. U.S. Department of State, *American Foreign Policy 1950-1955, Basic Documents* v. 1, U.S. Government Printing Office, Washington, p. 836.

out of our own hands. Our soldiers stationed in Europe, Japan, and Korea are hostages to insure our participation in any war started by a communist-ruled nation in those areas. Elsewhere where we have only a few troops, they too can involve us in a war just by being in place when hostilities begin.

Whether our previous actions were wise is beside the point. We took them to fit the situation of the late 1940s, which has vastly altered. Europe and Japan have become prosperous. Intercontinental ballistic missles have changed the character of war.

The two ways to prevent war are deterrence and avoidance. By our far-flung military presence we have put all our eggs in the basket of deterrence. Our statesmen's rhetoric about peace rings hollow when their disposition of our forces courts war.

There are no legal barriers to change. All our alliance treaties contain clauses that permit our cancellation of or withdrawal from the pacts after notice of one year or less except the Rio Pact, in which the notification required is two years.

Our allies are not to blame for the unfairness of our arrangements with them. To take what is offered is natural, especially when the recipient needs badly what is proffered. Our fault lies in ourselves. Our mistake is in continuing our stance after the conditions which prompted it no longer prevail.

To demonstrate the determination and nobility of the United States, our leaders have proclaimed that "the greatest nation on earth" will guard the world. For a nation of some 220,000,000, the burden is intolerable.

In addition to overburdening the fortitude of the American people, we are preparing for the wrong war in the wrong way. When the American people elect a president, they do not elect him as president of the world. Since 1947, however, each president has puffed up his office to "leader of the free world." Obedient to this direction our military establishment has been forced to keep step with the global inflation of our country's role. Irrespective of whether this has been the reason, in fact our major preparation has been for conventional wars overseas. Defense against nuclear war and invasion of the United States should come first.

The United States has capital and gross national product (GNP) tremendously larger than the USSR spread over fewer people, but militarily the Soviets are outspending us to an amazing degree. For fiscal year 1979 in constant dollars, the defense share of our GNP, of our total federal budget outlays, and of our net public spending decreased to only five-eights of the defense share for fiscal year 1964. If we spend proportionately only as much for the military as we did in fiscal 1964, we shall have no trouble in obtaining the money for additional nuclear arms. If we will not, it would seem that we must either raise taxes or curtail governmental domestic spending in order to obtain the nuclear money. But if in our military preparation we subordinate conventional war overseas to nuclear war, we can accomplish the apparently impossible; we can have our cake and eat it too.

We should increase rather than decrease our total defense budget, and we should not diminish our conventional forces. Everything that is said hereafter about disbanding some of them should be read in the light of this statement. But if Congress, representing the American people, will not vote increases in the whole defense budget, within its four corners Congress can nevertheless find the money to improve our safety greatly.

The popular supposition that the stupendous cost of nuclear weapons is the chief reason for our large military spending is a misconception. Of our total military outlays, only one eighth goes for nuclear arms and their manning; for every dollar we spend to prepare for nuclear war, we spend seven dollars to prepare for conventional war.[6] Hence, without increasing our total military expenditures, for every one-seventh decrease in our con-

---

6. *Annual Defense Department Report FY1981*, p. 123: "The total Department of Defense request for Strategic [nuclear] Offensive Forces in FY1981 is approximately $10.2 billion. This is about six percent of the DoD budget. Allocating overall support costs among functional areas gives an estimate of about 12 percent." *Annual Defense Department Report FY1977*, pp. 50-52, put the cost of nuclear forces at 10-15 percent of the whole military budget. Secretary of Defense James R. Schlesinger's *Statement before the Senate Armed Services Committee on the FY1975 Defense Budget and FY1974 Supplemental Request*, DOD, February 5, 1974, p. 15, said: "Strategic programs . . . for FY1975 come to only 8.4 percent of the total [military] budget, as compared to . . . in 1964 . . . 16.7 percent . . ."

ventional defense budget, we can double our nuclear budget without spending one additional dollar.

We must also maintain conventional forces to guard against invasion of the United States. To mount such an invasion, neither the USSR nor China has the naval or air transport vessels or the naval or air power to protect the transports against attack in transit; so the chance of such an invasion is remote. Still, Cuba, only 90 miles from our shores, has built up its military might, and we must think of later as well as sooner. Accordingly, any cut in our conventional war budget to gain additional nuclear strength must leave ample conventional arms and men to protect against invasion of our country.

For fiscal year 1979 Army and Marine Corps active duty personnel numbered 962,000. To aid them (excluding civilians performing duties not connected with defense) our Department of Defense employed 385,000 civilians.[7] Our ground forces stationed overseas cannot be counted on for defense against invasion because they are frozen in place by their missions and by the difficulty of transport to the United States during wartime. If brought back now, they still would have to be paid, fed, housed, and clothed unless disbanded. Therefore, to make a large saving we would have to bring home substantially all our ground forces and disband some of them. If our naval and air strength were not lessened, and if we concentrated in the United States practically all our active duty ground personnel and their civilian helpers, we could cut their numbers by half, and the United States still would be safe against invasion. The overhead of maintaining the men also would be cut in half, as would be the cost of equipping them. Even the most zealous advocates of conventional defense cannot validly dispute these propositions. Nor do they. They rest the need to keep our ground troops at their present level on the necessity to defend our allies and support a global posture.

As previously noted, a few thousand soldiers in each theater would have the same hostage character as hundreds of thousands. If to obtain the money to protect ourselves against nu-

7. *Annual Defense Manpower Requirements Report, FY1979*, pp. II, 1 and 3. The figures have not substantially changed.

clear war, we must withdraw practically all our troops overseas, we should.

We have lost sight of this simplicity by creating numerous policies and strategies, for which the military is not to blame. Whether we should continue to commit ourselves to the defense of more than 40 countries is beside the point for the Pentagon, which must prepare according to our commitments as long as they subsist.

Commentators on foreign affairs stress strategy. An idea, however, does not become profound by calling it strategic. Among the difficulties in using the art of strategy are the differences among its expounders about its principles and their application. Granted that strategy will continue to play a role in the nuclear age, strategy has not always determined the outcome of wars. Superior numbers, tactics, morale, training of troops, choice of lieutenants, and luck all have played prominent parts, as has superiority in weapons. B. H. Liddell Hart, who championed the indirect approach, attributed Count H. J. L. von Moltke's 1866 victory over the Austrians despite the "direct approach [of the Prussians] with little trace of guile," to the inferiority of the Austrian muzzle-loader against the Prussian breech-loading rifle.[8] In a nuclear war the relative quantity and quality of weapons are likely to be decisive. For deterring nuclear war the same principle holds true.

It is not only bad generals who fight the last war; the same tendency afflicts good generals and statesmen; for the wars they have lived through remain most vivid to them. Most of our policies and strategies have three common characteristics: (1) They refight World War II without the atom bomb. (2) In doing so they posit the necessity of our overseas presence. (3) Based on that assumption they justify the policy or strategy.

Our "forward strategy" illustrates the tendency. Once it is conceded that we must keep a large number of American troops in Germany, a forward strategy by positioning them there in peacetime is sensible; for in wartime it would be difficult to re-

8. B. H. L. Hart, *Strategy*, Frederick A. Praeger, New York, 1967, pp. 154-155.

inforce by transporting soldiers and munitions across an ocean prowled by Soviet submarines, and our airlift is limited. The fault is in the initial assumption.

Our troops in West Germany, Japan, and Korea do not protect us against invasion from Cuba, Canada, or Mexico, and we can better deter and defend against a conventional invasion of the United States by stationing our soldiers in our homeland. Our navy in American waters, our air force brought home, and our nuclear weapons would provide a real forward defense of the United States against invasion. Despite the forward presence of our troops, Soviet nuclear missiles can hit the United States. Because of our forward presence, Soviet nuclear missiles are more likely to be launched against the United States. In fact, our forward strategy is not designed to protect the United States against invasion; it is fashioned to protect our allies.

Such failures to go to the roots of survival and peace in the nuclear age have led us not only to prepare for the wrong war, but to prepare in the wrong way, as illustrated by our strategy of "flexible graduated response." The chance that a Soviet-American war would not start or become nuclear is almost nil. To Soviet military officers and writers it seems ridiculous to suppose that in a war between adversaries with large nuclear arsenals, neither will use them. In contrast, flexible graduated response clings to the hope that a Soviet-American war will remain conventional. Should the USSR attack with conventional forces in Europe, we say that NATO would first defend with conventional arms; if NATO were losing, we would next use tactical (short-range) nuclear weapons stationed in Europe; if we were still losing, we would launch our strategic (long-range) nuclear missiles. The USSR has read all our statements. Even if it believes us, which it does not, it hardly will be enchanted by the advantages to it of a conventional war that will remain conventional only if the Soviets are losing.

Two inescapable facts undermine graduated flexible response: the obvious advantage of the first nuclear blow and our possession of the only formidable nuclear arsenal in the noncommunist world. None of our allies has a nuclear arsenal except Britain and France, and theirs are insignificant when compared to ours.

Flexible graduated response is a strategy that neglects the obvious: Concurrently with or preceeding any attack on NATO forces in Europe, the USSR almost certainly will make a first nuclear strike on the United States. The Soviets must to prevent our having the advantage of the first nuclear blow with our full nuclear arsenal, undisabled by prior attack, and without our being demoralized by an attack on our population.

It may be granted that there is a possibility or even a capability that the Soviets will attack in Europe without using nuclear weapons. If the United States and its NATO allies were willing to spend unlimited money and have many more men under arms equipped with enough tanks and everything else that money can buy plus unlimited nuclear missiles, we might justify preparing for the unlikely contingency, but that is not the case. One fault of pushing the doctrine of capabilities in peacetime to its outer bounds is that in trying to prepare against everything, we prepare well against nothing.

Nor are our policies and strategies immaterial even if they will be jettisoned the instant war begins. They hurt us now and will hurt us even more in the event of war because they affect how we prepare to avoid, deter, and defend. Besides enough trained men with excellent weapons, the essence of preparing in the right way consists of two elements: force structure and disposition. In these regards our strategies are deleterious to us. Pursuant to them, we spend so much money preparing for a conventional war overseas that our nuclear preparation suffers, and we have placed our men overseas so as to insure that the United States will be a belligerent in any Soviet-Western European war. As a result of our strategies, in the event of such a war the United States is the magnet of a Soviet first strike. Having accomplished this undesirable state of affairs, we have stripped our people of shelter and shield.

To point out that the only wars we have fought since World War II have been conventional wars in Korea and Vietnam does not uphold our strategies. The American people are sensibly unwilling to fight such a war again. But the more basic answer is that only when we have prepared ourselves to be as safe as reasonably possible against nuclear war should we prepare for other wars. Our force structure and dispositions should correspond to this principle.

Aside from containment of communism, our chief policy to justify our global military presence has been "collective security." The policy is collective only in name because the burden sharing is not in proportion to ability to carry. Nor is the policy secure. Under it we have no nuclear shelter, have interred our shield, and have shrunk our deterrent.

In defense of collective security as manifested by our presence in Europe, our State and Defense Departments emphasize the benefit to us from adding many European men and weapons to our own. That begs the vital question: Who is defending whom? We are in no danger of a Soviet invasion; it is our European allies that are in such peril. And the threat of a Soviet nuclear attack on the United States arises primarily because our nuclear arsenal protects our European allies.

Most strategists begin their discourse on their art with the stern command: Look at the map. This is sensible if we are to fight an overseas conventional war, particularly in Asia, because ships and aircraft still need bases. Before we thus look at the map, however, we ought to decide whether we should fight another such war and whether we are willing to do so.

Before we "lost" Indochina, we called ourselves an Asian power. Since then, in our own words we have deftly become a "North Asian" or "Northeastern Asian" power, and in 1978 Jimmy Carter affirmed our unswerving determination to remain such a power because of our "national interest." That phrase covers a multitude of sins against it. Basically, national interest translates into our paramount aim of survival as a free people and our secondary aim of prosperity, which overseas means trade. Apart from the fact that our primary aim should take precedence over our secondary objective, to promote trade we need neither alliances nor military presence nor bases. Without any, nations will trade with us if trade is profitable for them. From 1798 to 1941 our overseas commerce required neither alliances nor troops stationed abroad. Presently, without either, Sweden profitably trades overseas. West Germany and Japan, which trade all over the world, keep their forces at home. Our national interest in northeast Asia consists of our obligations to defend Japan, the Philippines, and South Korea by war against an attack by China, or the Soviet Union, or North Korea.

The 1979 Soviet invasion of Afghanistan evoked a search by the Carter administration for American bases on the Horn of Africa, in the Indian Ocean, and near the Persian Gulf. But for years the Soviets have had the conventional military power to seize the Persian Gulf states, including Iran. A glance at the map and a contemplation of the logistics show the folly of an American conventional war against the USSR in this area bordering its homeland and some 7,000 miles away from ours. When in his 1980 State of the Union message President Carter said that we would use "military force" against "an attempt by any outside force [the USSR is obviously meant] to gain control of the Persian Gulf region," he was threatening either a conventional war we cannot win or nuclear war.

The proposed bases would neither insure our supply of oil from the Persian Gulf nor cheapen the price of the oil we buy. The bases and the military personnel who would man them, however, would be expensive and would increase the chance of our involvement in war.

The American people are small in number compared to the Asiatics but are technologically advanced in weapons and capable in the air and on the seas. Under these circumstances, a strategy that prepares to fight another conventional war on the mainland of Asia must be a mistake.

While studying the map, the strategist also should remember the state of science and technology when he looks. After steam replaced sail, the British picked up coaling stations all over the world. It was not the map which prompted the decision; it was the new invention. The map after nuclear weapons is not the same as the map before.

The map, though seemingly the same, is not really the same in peace as in war. When we were subsidizing Portugal in its resistance to the rebellion of its African colonies, some strategists approved and pointed out that if Mozambique, on the east coast of Africa, were in hostile hands, tankers from the Persian

Gulf would have to sail by 1,000 miles of hostile shores at great peril. Mozambique fell to the communists, and the tankers still sail by. If a Soviet-American war comes, they will not sail by the east coast of Africa even if Mozambique is in friendly hands; they will have been stopped at the Persian Gulf. The Mozambique exercise repeated a favorite strategical disquisition in justification of faraway bases that we now hold or should add. The strategist enumerates the number of tankers carrying oil to Europe and the United States that pass daily through the Persian Gulf. Then he traces their route along the eastern shore of Africa and a-round the Cape of Good Hope in South Africa. It is curious that our strategists do not mention that in the event of a Soviet-American-European war the USSR could stop the tankers at their loading points by air power from its home territory. Just how we would protect the Persian Gulf oil source against a major enemy during war, even with a strong base in the Indian Ocean or on the Horn of Africa, the strategists have not deigned to enlighten us. But they continue to stress the dangers of hostile control of the Indian Ocean, African coasts, and the littorals of "strategic" straits such as the straits of Malacca. In peacetime such control makes no difference; the ships are going to sail by or through whoever controls the shores. In nuclear war with the Soviet Union, the argument would become academic.

It may be granted that both during peacetime and during conventional war it would be desirable for us to have such littorals in friendly hands. But a strategy is worthless unless it answers the question: By what tool? We have tried propping up incompetent governments with subsidies, from which our home front has suffered in fortitude because of the character of the governments we have supported. In doing so we have become the champion of the status quo and stability in a world of ferment. And additional countries still have become communist-ruled. Chapter 8 will discuss the appropriate tool by which to win back communist-ruled countries that seem necessary to us, and the tool is not war or subsidy. In this regard "No more Vietnams" is a sensible slogan that the American people are going to abide by whatever the strategists say.

Strategic writing justifies far-flung bases, military presence, and power to be projected by large aircraft carriers because of our necessity to have access to vital raw materials. The same reason is advanced for a strong navy to keep the sea lanes open in wartime. Whether we need large aircraft carriers or many smaller naval vessels is a debate that may be passed, and inherent uncertainty is a sufficient ground for a strong navy. Naval vessels, however, can produce no raw materials; they can only try to convoy merchant fleets carrying the raw materials, and against Soviet submarines the outcome would be dubious. Some of our most critical materials come from southern Africa, where we have no bases or presence. Stockpiling critical materials and developing substitutes for them is cheaper and less dangerous to peace than our global presence.

In looking at the map, our strategists see the Mediterranean as a "Soviet lake" without the presence of our Sixth Fleet and shore bases to maintain it. To show the flag for the encouragement of the faint-hearted, the Sixth Fleet could appear in the Mediterranean from time to time without bases. If the Sixth Fleet were to fight a conventional war in the Mediterranean, our present bases would be a great aid. But the only major nation with which we would fight such a war is the Soviet Union, and it is carrying optimism to its outer bounds to suppose that such a war would not become nuclear. Our Mediterranean bases have some value for nuclear war; they are convenient for carriers and submarines. The submarines, however, could operate without the bases, and carrier-based aircraft are a small factor in our total nuclear deterrent.

Defense Department reports argue for our Mediterranean presence and our bases in Italy, Turkey, and Greece to protect NATO's south and southeastern flanks. The whole idea of flanks is inapplicable to nuclear war; nuclear missiles do not need to collapse flanks. If we had no commitment to protect Italy, it would not be our flank in conventional war. The same is true of Greece and Turkey. The danger of communist rule in Italy arises not from the threat of external aggression, but from the incompetent government which Italy has suffered. Turkey and Greece may become neutral if we withdraw our protection, but they are not going to become communist to spite us.

Another argument advanced for our Mediterranean bases is resupplying Israel in the next Arab war. But it would be far cheaper in money and danger to give Israel an ample reserve of munitions than to maintain men and bases in Europe for a resupply.

Because of their geographic position, Denmark and Norway, "NATO's northern flank," are said to be a cork in the Baltic bottle. Soviet submarines from the Baltic would be at sea before the Soviets started a war. Moreover, the submarines now being deployed by the Soviet Union have a range sufficient to hit the continental United States without leaving the Baltic. Denmark has an insignificant army and could be seized easily by the USSR. The Norwegians have a better army but could not hold out until reinforcements arrived; the Soviet deployment in the North is overwhelming. In all probability the whole idea of a northern flank in a European conventional war is fantasy; a European war with the USSR will become nuclear.

In the nuclear age and long after the liquidation of all the colonial empires except that of the USSR, our strategists are using the same words that Europeans used when they were grabbing as many territories overseas as they could lay their hands on. Among the words to justify our military presence in faraway places, the shadowy word "influence" ranks high. Whatever may have been the morality of colonialism and imperialism, at least the Europeans knew what they were striving for: money or resources which produced money. Influence does a nation no good unless converted to material benefits. When the British or French sought a sphere of influence or a protectorate, they expected it to pay by mining concessions, plantations, or other lucrative rewards. Our influence, if we have it, costs us large sums with nothing tangible in return. This is not an argument for imperialism; it is an argument against our military presence overseas.

In current usage "isolation" and "fortress America" have become code words to describe a benighted condition to which the United States must never return. We did well with isolation during most of our history. Without our global military presence, we will not be isolated in trade or cultural exchange. Isolation by not having troops abroad avoids war; their presence is unnecessary to deter war. The United States with a stronger nuclear offensive arsenal than we now have plus civil and active defense is our best deterrent to nuclear war, and shelter and shield are the indispensable means of our survival if nuclear war comes.

Because our global military presence has been dressed in the clothes of peace, perhaps a majority of the American people support the policy, but sooner or later Vietnam predicts the collapse of our posture on the home front. Wise statesmanship anticipates. While there are persuasive arguments against withdrawing our troops, when weighed on the scale of judgment, it tips in favor of bringing the boys back home.

Our abrupt departure would leave our allies in the lurch and would be neither decent nor in our own interest. The pace of withdrawal should give time to train Europeans as replacements for our soldiers. Nor can we expect West Germany, the front line country, to deter or defend without nuclear weapons.

Allowing West Germany to acquire nuclear weapons is not enough. Without our nuclear knowledge it would take West Germany too long to catch up, and unnecessary economic hardship would be imposed on the West Germans. Starting from scratch, it took France many years of scientific and technological effort and an investment of more than $25 billion to create the small French nuclear arsenal.

Having accustomed our European allies to our protection, if we are to withdraw, we must proffer them a fair subsititue. The proposal should be public and subjected to debate on both sides of the Atlantic. Without payment to us, we should offer West Germany, Britain, France, The Netherlands, and Belgium our nuclear knowledge in exchange for an agreement whereby West Germany would create a strong nuclear arsenal, Britain and France would enlarge and improve theirs, and The Netherlands and Belgium would help under a sharing arrangement. Whether other North Atlantic Treaty Organization (NATO) countries would be included would be resolved within European NATO, subject to our approval. While the nuclear arming is in progress, we would agree to hold our nuclear umbrella over Europe but would withdraw our conventional forces at an agreed rate to be replaced with European conventional forces. For discussion with our friends, many items, including the timetable, would be left open in the original offer, but with these irreducible minimums: When the transition period is completed, all American forces must be out of Europe, and western Europe must have created a strong nuclear arsenal. Keeping our men in Europe during the transition period would be conditioned upon European performance according to an agreed schedule.

The presence of our troops so comforts our allies that unless the alternative is plainly stated, they may reject the proposal. We should therefore add: It would be less than fair not to tell you that if you reject our proposal, we will terminate the North Atlantic Treaty, withdraw our nuclear umbrella, and bring home all our forces from Europe.

Under the probable timetable, one-fifth of our troops would come home a year from acceptance and our last men would leave Europe within five years. The completion of west European nuclear arming probably would take ten years.

Upon us the accepted proposal would confer immense benefits. With the creation of other powerful nuclear arsenals, we would stop being the sole Soviet magnet target. At the conclusion of the transition period, our troops would be home with the consequent increased chance of avoiding an American war. The conventional deterrent would not decrease; Europeans would replace Americans. The total nuclear deterrent would be greatly increased, and not only in Europe. With the money saved, we could increase our own nuclear arsenal. To be sure, the USSR might respond by increasing its nuclear arms, but there is a limit to its ability to match. One of the gravest flaws in the present arrangement is its failure to use western Europe to the extent of its capacity.

Acceptance of the proposal also would greatly benefit western Europe. It now relies upon a military presence by the United States which is not likely to last because of its unfairness to us. In their own interest the Europeans should not wait until we decide to pull out; for if the future be judged by the past, our retreat will be hasty. Successive resolutions proposed by former

Senator Michael J. Mansfield (Montana) to bring part of our troops home from Europe were defeated; someday a bill to bring all our boys back home may pass.

The support of our present posture by Congress and the media should not greatly comfort our allies. At the start and in the early years of our fighting in Vietnam, Congress was for the war; the few voices against were lost in the favorable volume. Senator George McGovern (South Dakota), who later inveighed against the immorality of our Vietnamese War, spoke and voted for the war initially. Our metropolitan newspapers and television networks that became opponents of the war were its enthusiastic supporters at the outset. Dependent as our allies are on our protection, they run the fearful risk of a sudden veering of sentiment in the United States.

When the interim period is over, for the first time since World War II western Europe will not have to look across the Atlantic and wonder. Europe will again be master of its own destiny and with better protection than now.

Charles de Gaulle perceived that the European-American relationship was unnatural. He did not expect American troops to remain in Europe. In the event of a Soviet assault on Europe, he saw that the American monopoly of nuclear weapons gave the United States the choice of betrayal or its own devastation. De Gaulle was right; a Europe that for its protection totally depends on us is in a precarious position.

Our European allies have not acted like client states; under our tolerant protection they have done more or less at they pleased. But as long as they rely on us for their nuclear deterrent and defense, they are dependent states. In the future our polite suggestions may alter to a command to do as we say or take the consequences. This is not a happy state of affairs for proud nations with glorious pasts and the resources, brains, and skills for glorious futures. On both sides of the Atlantic some have openly voiced a doubt that others harbor in secret: In the event of a Warsaw Pact conventional invasion or of a Soviet nuclear attack on Europe without an attack on the United States, would the United States respond?

The size of our deterrent is subject to the vagaries of our

domestic politics. Each American presidential election causes Europe to shiver. Although every American president has reassured our allies of our unshakable resolve, there is a strong antimilitarist tradition in our history, not to mention that for most of it we cherished our isolation from Europe. Woodrow Wilson won the election of 1916 on the plank: He kept us out of war. It took the Japanese attack to induce us to enter World War II. The Vietnamese War has soured the American people on foreign involvements. In short, western Europe will be as secure as it can expect to be in a dangerous world only when it assumes the burden of its own deterrence and defense. And in a nuclear world, that means strong nuclear arsenals.

If West Germany confederated with England, France, or either of them, the proposal could be consummated without violation of the Nuclear Nonproliferation Treaty.[9] But because confederation is unlikely, the proposal must envision termination of the pact. This would be no disaster; the treaty has served only to spread nuclear knowledge, and with its short cancellation clause the pact is no bar to a signatory's becoming a nuclear power.

It begs the question, however, to discuss only the treaty. Our reasons for opposing spread deserve a fair statement. We now have to guard against only one formidable nuclear arsenal; once we abandon this policy we may have to guard against many. Even if nuclear weapons are going to spread sooner or later, later is better for us than sooner. Before and during World War II Germany and Japan were aggressive nations. Frequently today's allies have become tomorrow's enemies. Someday a nation to which we give our nuclear knowledge may launch its missiles against us.

To characterize our fear of a shift of alliances as chimeric would be to disown the patterns of history. But without the spread of nuclear weapons to the West Germans we cannot bring all our troops home to avoid an American war. Nor can we create other strong nuclear arsenals as deterrents or remove ourselves as the sole magnet target. For everything we pay a price. In peril for us the price of denying West Germany nuclear weapons is too high to pay.

9. U.S. Arms Control and Disarmament Agency, *Arms Control and Disarmament Agreements*, U.S. Government Printing Office, Washington, 1975, p. 82.

The state of internal politics in Italy and France is a good reason against giving either nation our nuclear knowledge. We cannot rely on safeguards or promises that communists in government will have no access to the information we transmit; all such paper chains are untrustworthy. Probably Italy will present no problem; it will take a good many years before it is willing to spend considerably more money on defense. France is a more difficult case because it will spend the money and may have a government in which the French Communist Party participates. If we decided to confine the offer to England, West Germany, and the Low Countries, the decision would be understandable, but realistically it probably will be impossible to exclude France.

The fear that our nuclear sercrets will leak from our allies to the USSR is easily allayed. We would furnish our allies only with such knowledge as the Soviets already have. This would protect any areas in which we have the lead, yet put the Germans, French, and English on an even basis with the USSR.

That bringing home our forces is what the USSR has sought should give us pause. But it has assumed that if we withdraw, the West Germans will not have nuclear weapons, the English and French nuclear arsenals will not be augmented, and American troops brought home will not be replaced by Europeans. The USSR hardly would be happy about a doubling of the total nuclear arsenals of its adversaries, nor would it jump with joy over the increase in European conventional strength.

One of the main obstacles to European acceptance will be economic; survival ought to take precedence but not always has. West Germany should bear the heaviest burden; it is the front line country and the wealthiest. If forced to, West Germany could shoulder the whole load, but there is no reason to suppose that it would have to; the other western European countries would help because they need German soldiers and resources for European defense.

We should leave our allies no room to doubt that if the proposal is rejected, our men will be brought home and our nuclear protection withdrawn. Faced with that alternative, the West Germans in the front line would have little choice. Even if they had to make a bilateral agreement with the United States, in all likelihood they would. France would not relish nuclear inferiority to West Germany; so probably France, helped by our nuclear knowledge, also would increase its nuclear arsenal greatly.

It is too much to expect a confederation for defense and foreign affairs among Britain, France, West Germany, and the Low Countries. Necessity, however, may father the child. If it did, the safety of western Europe and the United States would increase.

Concerning our future participation in the alliance, it is possible to differ reasonably. Eventually, the United States should cooperate with western Europe but not be allied to it in order to avoid American involvement in a European war. But we have to think of the reaction of our allies. Accordingly, if the proposal is accepted, we should be willing to forgo our right to terminate during the transition period. After that, the one year withdrawal clause of the North Atlantic Treaty now in force should apply.

If during discussion on both sides of the Atlantic it became apparent that the proposal had a good chance of consummation, would the USSR refuse to tolerate a West Germany with its own nuclear weapons? Phrases like "refuse to tolerate" need annotation with the question: By what tool? Probably the Soviets would propagandize, strive to stir internal agitation against the proposal, and try to seduce by diplomacy. But would they start a war because the Soviet position vis-a-vis western Europe would be weaker after the transition period than before? No one can be sure that the Soviet leadership would refrain from war if the proposal seemed to be winning favor. It is equally true that no one can be sure that the Soviet leadership will refrain from war without the proposal. There is the capability in either case. If we defer the proposal because we are afraid it would lead to a Soviet war, we should largely increase our nuclear arsenal; for our fear of making the proposal would have demonstrated our realization of the inadequacy of our deterrent.

There are traditional divisions among Europeans. Our allies may doubt their ability to deter or resist without the presence of our troops. Hence, they may reject the proposal, elect to become neutral, and to do as the Soviets force them to do.

Although strategists have shuddered at the prospect, such so-called Finlandization would not jeopardize American objectives.

Our survival would be helped; for it is threatened only by nuclear war, and our chance of avoiding such a war would be enhanced because the confrontation at the point of friction would have been removed. Our deterrent would increase rather than lessen. True, there would be subtracted from the total nuclear deterrent the British and French arsenals, but as a percentage of allied strength they are small. The loss would be more than offset by our increase in nuclear arms from the money saved by bringing home our conventional forces and disbanding some of them. Nor would our secondary aim of national prosperity be affected. Europe needs American trade as much as we need European trade.

The most serious objection to the proposal arises from imagining the worst case, the conquest by the Soviet Union of western Europe following the latter's Finlandization. The next chapter will point out the danger to us if the USSR succeeds in changing many countries not communist-ruled to countries ruled by communist parties. But that peril to us would arise from communist rule by internal subversion aided by external subversion, and the last chapter will also note the difficulties the USSR would have in holding a communist bloc together.

Imposition of communist rule by conquest would give rise to a far different situation. In the long run such a conquest would bring the overthrow of all European communist governments, including that of the USSR. No conqueror in ancient, medieval, or modern history ever has been able to rule Europe for long. A conquered Europe would inflict upon the Soviet Union a fatal case of acute indigestion. It is hard enough now for the USSR to hold its satellites in line; it would be impossible in the case of a conquered Europe. The nations of western Europe that have known freedom would be in perpetual revolt.

Nor by its conquest would the rest of Europe acquire additional nuclear weapons. The USSR would fear that western European troops might turn the nuclear weapons on the Soviet Union. In short, even the worst case would not jeopardize our paramount objective.

Although the worst case would not be fatal to us in the long run, the short run would create a miserable situation that we should strive to prevent. The worst case, however, is highly improbable. Western Europe is not going to become communist in pique or to spite us. It would not be Americans who would live under Soviet oppressive rule; it would be western Europeans. They have created a civilization of which they are justly proud; they will not easily surrender it to the barbarians. The western Europeans have not been cravens. To believe that they would choose to submit is to deny the whole history of these brave people. In all likelihood they will resume their natural self-reliance if we remove the crutch.

Granted that there is still the capability of surrender, the competing capabilities weigh heavily on the scale of judgment. Our present situation is perilous to us both for avoidance and for deterrence. Nor will it endure; it is too obviously unfair to the American people. The chance that they will become impatient and force a precipitate retreat also counts on the scale. All the worst features of the worst case would be aggravated by our sudden retreat without the protective elements contained in the proposal.

Even if the USSR moves its divisions now facing China to the Soviet western front, the western Europeans will be in less danger than now if they have strong nuclear arsenals. Anything is possible, but a Soviet conventional attack on a West Europe armed with potent nuclear weapons almost certainly would bring a nuclear response. The sooner we and our allies accept the fact, as the Soviets do, that any general European war will be nuclear, the sooner preparation will be in accordance. All formidable western European nuclear forces need is a conventional shield that allows time for nuclear missiles to be launched. Flexible graduated response is an armchair strategy not likely to be followed in war.

The argument that we must defend Europe, no matter how unfair are the arrangements, neglects the way people act. European civilization is indeed our priceless heritage, but we cannot and will not preserve it in Europe unless the Europeans themselves show an equal willingness. If they put their temporary prosperity ahead of their saftey, no one will save them.

The proposed plan is radical in both senses of the word: it goes to the root and advocates an extreme change. But our situation has become more and more precarious, and prudence is not synonomous with lack of change. Granted that there are persuasive arguments against the plan, on a fair judgment, our danger is greater from our present posture.

Practically everything that has been said about western Europe applies to Japan; repeating would be tedious. To the Japanese, we should be less generous about expense and timing than to the Europeans, not because the Japanese are less worthy, but because our bargain with them has been completely one-sided, and because as a pacifist nation, Japan contributes next to nothing to its own defense and nothing to the defense of the United States. Nevertheless, having accustomed Japan to our protection, decency requires giving it the time and opportunity to develop its own substitute. It is ironic that the Japanese have expressed concern about the decline of our capacity to protect them. Some of our hawks fear that unless we do better, the Japanese will seek another protector, and that as a quid pro quo they will sell the product of their tremendous manufacturing capacity to our communist-ruled enemies. This assumes that the Japanese are fools, which certainly they are not. They will neither forsake their lucrative American market nor throw themselves into the embrace of their communist enemies close to their own shores to get even with us or because of irritation with us.

The apprehension that China will again become a Soviet ally because the Chinese will read our European proposal as a sign of weakness has no validity. The consummated proposal would array greater strength against the USSR, which is what China wants. The Chinese, however, will not welcome our withdrawal from Asia, where they consider our military presence a deterrent to a Soviet attack on China. But both the Chinese and the Soviets know that if the USSR attacks China, we will not risk our own nuclear destruction to save China. Nor have we promised to do so. And if there is an American deterrent to a Soviet assault on China, the real deterrent is not our inadequate ground and air forces in Japan and Korea; the real deterrent is our nuclear arsenal, which would still exist. In all likelihood China will decide whether to mend the Sino-Soviet schism without regard for whatever we do. Granted that China is somewhat more likely to do so if we leave Asia, the risk is worth taking. Our Asian presence has far less justification than our European. Moreover, if we retain our bases in the Philippines, the Chinese probably will be sufficiently assured.

South Korea is much larger in population than North Korea and not inferior in resources. During the more than a quarter century since the Korean War we have fully discharged any obligation that we had. If North Korea attacks, it would be regrettable, but the South Koreans should be capable of handling it alone. Let them fight it out. The presence of our troops is a deterrent in favor of South Korea, but the price of the deterrent is too high in terms of avoidance. The American people are unwilling to fight another Korean War, but by the presence of American troops we would be in any such war, like it or not. By fighting the Korean War we did not appoint ourselves the guardian of South Korea forever. But let us err on the side of fairness by supplying South Korea with advanced conventional weapons on generous terms or partially as gifts. Having put South Korea in a position equal to North Korea in weapons, we should bring *all* our forces home and end the alliance after giving South Korea ample time to add troops and weapons for its own defense.

We have jettisoned Taiwan with the approval of our European allies. If they are wise, they will see our abandonment of Taiwan both as a repetition of the customary conduct of nations and as a portent that should lead Europe to create its own nuclear defense. The only objection to Jimmy Carter's cancellation of our defense treaty with Taiwan pursuant to its one-year termination clause was his method. The American people are sensibly unwilling to fight a war for the defense of an Asian island. But in decency we should give Taiwan enough nuclear knowledge to enable it to put itself on an equal nuclear footing wth China, and we should also supply Taiwan with advanced conventional weapons. China will resent our arming Taiwan but will respect us for so doing. The reason for the arming is not realpolitik; it is honor. Even those who disliked our original and long continued commitment should not forget that we made it. At least we should give the people of Taiwan the means to defend their island.

V. I. Lenin believed that because of the vast population of

Asia, the ideology that prevailed on that continent would win the world. But Lenin's tool for winning Asia was subversion, not war. We have neither the will nor the manpower to defend Asian countries against communism by conventional war, and we are not going to wage nuclear war to do so. If additional Asian countries become communist, we should supply dissidents with money and, when propitious, with arms.

If "a foolish consistency is the hobgoblin of little minds," inconsistency becomes sensible when circumstances indicate a proper exception to a rule. Retaining American bases in the Philippines would be valuable for deterrence and would hurt our avoidance of war only minimally; for the islands are far enough away from the mainland so that our forces do not confront the USSR or China. Moreover, keeping the bases would soften the blow for China of our Asian withdrawal.

Similarly, there is no objection to American Pacific island bases or to island bases elsewhere, and particularly where they are necessary for surveillance or tracking of Soviet missiles. Where bases do not hurt our avoidance of war situation, the rule of withdrawal should not be applied; for its reason does not exist.

Variations of the precise proposals set forth are possible. The criteria already noted should determine their worth.

At bottom the error in our thinking has been playing balance of power politics, which always has ended in war, in a world where a nuclear war would be disastrous. Pursuant to such an approach, we have regarded the United States as a superpower with client states to be propitiated and never offended lest they defect to the enemy. If we need allies, we need those that will share fairly both our financial burdens and our danger. It was generous but in our own interest to donate the money to rebuild a western Europe ravaged by two world wars; for our statesmen to continue to place on the shoulders of the American people burdens that western Europe and Japan, recovered and prosperous, are capable of carrying themselves is a grave error. If our allies have not the will to protect themselves, they are beyond our power to help. But from the history of western Europe and Japan, these courageous and able nations will fend for themselves if they must and if we offer them the nuclear knowledge to enable them to stand on their own feet. In the interest of our allies and ourselves, it is time to require them to do so.

When we remember that until the late 1940s and the early 1950s our present policies and strategies would have been considered alien to the American tradition, and when we realize that our policies and strategies make our involvement in war more likely, it is not heretical to assail our present orthodoxy. In the light of our paramount aim our catchphrase policies and strategies are not a proper American preparedness theology; they are rank heresies.

* * * * *

Chapters 2-5 suggest armed might as our prime tool for survival and peace, with defense added to deterrence, and with diplomacy in an auxiliary role. Chapter 6 suggests avoidance of war by bringing the boys back home, but with fairness to our allies. The last two chapters concern subversion, the most reviled tool, which can be an instrument of our survival and peace.

CHAPTER 7

The Double-Pronged Conflict

"There are, at the present time, two great nations in the world, which seem to tend towards the same end, although they started from different points: I allude to the Russians and the Americans. . . . All other nations seem to have nearly reached their natural limits, . . . but these are still in the act of growth . . . The American . . . gives free scope to the unguided exertions and common sense of the citizens; the Russian centers all the authority of society in a single arm: the principal instrument of the former is freedom; of the latter, servitude. Their starting point is different, and their courses are not the same; yet each of them seems to be marked out by the will of Heaven to sway the destinies of half the globe."[1] These lines were written in 1835 by Alexis de Tocqueville. Even his remarkable prescience did not foresee the new breed of Russian tyrants who attempt to impose the rule of communist masters not on half, but on the whole globe. Their instrument is a conflict that pierces by double prongs: One is subversion; the other is war.

According to Karl Marx and Friedrich Engels, the conflict is inescapable. Their theory reduces man to an economic animal and compresses history into a single mold of struggle between successive dominant and oppressed economic classes, culminating at each stage in the violent overthrow of the dominant class.

The conflict proceeds unevenly because nations develop unevenly. Russia and Asia, still in the feudal stage, must first have bourgeois revolutions and then proletarian revolutions. But, Marx

1. A. de Tocqueville, *Democracy in America*, v. 1, 1835, concluding two paragraphs.

125

and Engels said, the advanced capitalist countries such as France, Germany, and England were ripe for the proletarian revolution.

Although the motive impelling the class struggle is economic, the action in each country is through the violent capture of state power by the oppressed class. The future history of the struggle is scientifically inevitable, Marx and Engels asserted, but men must help it along. With this assistance, the last act of the historical drama will bring victory over the capitalist class to the proletariat, followed by communism. Under its beneficent reign, all mankind will become good and dwell happily in a materialist garden of Eden with God left out; for there is no God, and religion has been only the opium of the people. The Marxian play has a class murder as the climax of each act except the last. Had Shakespeare written the last act, his characters would have killed each other in a quarrel over the division of the spoils.

There is a grain of truth in Marxism. In *The Federalist* (No. 10), long before either Marx or Engels was born, James Madison in his discourse on the causes of faction "sown in the nature of man" wrote: "The most common and durable source of factions has been the various and unequal distribution of property." But Madison also ascribed the animosities in society to other causes, among them religion, form of government, attachment to different contending leaders, ambitions, human passions, and "the most frivolous and fanciful distinctions."

Many learned writers have exposed historical errors of Marx and Engels. To repeat that exercise here would serve no purpose; for although V. I. Lenin swallowed whole the Marxian ideology and theory of history, and although Lenin also thought that the conflict was unavoidable, he twisted through Marxist rigidity to create a system of action for himself and his heirs to follow.

The plan of the communist-ruled states and its intended manner of execution are inscrutable only because the obvious is the easiest to overlook. In penetrating the unenigmatic enigma, the study of Lenin is the alpha and omega. Trying to distill the essence of communist doctrine abroad without a thorough knowledge of Lenin is like attempting to understand Christianity without reading any of the four gospels. Studying Marx and Engels, while helpful, is not a requisite. Although Lenin cited Engels almost as frequently as Marx, communist doctrine usually is called Marxism-Leninism. It should be called Leninism because the working theory of the Soviet Union has been and still is what Lenin said Marx and Engels meant with Lenin's additions.

Soviet and communist Chinese comment on Lenin is never criticism; the comment is confined to exegesis of his voluminous writings and speeches and to an attempt to understand his actions in gaining and holding power. His words and deeds, sacrosanct in the communist world, comprise the bible of communist doctrine. Nor is it a bible laid on the upper shelf and forgotten. Soviet discussion of any subject nearly always drags in Lenin. Practically every professional article by a Soviet military man cites and often quotes a passage from Lenin. His words and deeds are taught in every Soviet school, and with veneration. In the west Lenin may seem outmoded; in the communist world he is the key to its thinking.

Lenin's multitudinous words, when read in the context of the occasions for their utterance and as a whole, form reasonably simple and consistent themes into which his deeds fit. Lenin was not a hypocrite. Since he told with little equivocation what the communists intend to do, and since his heirs follow his precepts, there is no excuse for poohpoohing their purposes.

"Stalinism" is misleading. Lenin originated Soviet cruelty, terror, and oppression, including the prison camps, as scholars long have known; Alexandr I. Solzhenitsyn has stilled any lingering doubt. In relation to our paramount aim, however, the core is Leninism abroad, whose distinctive features are simple.

The objective is to place communist parties in control of all governments. The area is the globe. The expected duration of the struggle to accomplish the objective is very protracted.

The chief tactics are: Keep trying. Be governed by the situation. Use the "zigzag"; when strong, attack; when weak, retreat until strength is regained. Dissemble to confuse the adversary, the bourgeois nations. In the course of the long struggle, make temporary concessions to obtain the needs of the Soviet Union from the capitalist nations, but take them back as soon as feasible. Finally, do not believe that communist parties can gain and hold control of governments by legal peaceful means; use violence, which is indispensable to success. "And," Lenin said, "in the twentieth century — as in the age of civilization generally — violence means neither a fist nor a club, but *troops*."[2]

The first piercing prong of communism is subversion. Preparatory subversion, chiefly by propaganda and agitation, is to be steadily carried on. In turn preparatory subversion sets the stage for decisive subversions designed to overthrow all bourgeois governments by force. The subversions are to be executed by an internal communist nucleus and aided externally by communist-ruled states.

The other piercing prong is war. Lesser implements are diplomacy, political treaties, and trade to gain time and strength in the course of the struggle for the ultimate blow by force. Varied though communist tactics may seem according to place, time, and circumstances, this summary and Lenin's attitude to war — discussed in Chapter 2 — cover the simple essence of Leninism abroad.

Lenin's heirs have thought and still think the same. On the protracted double-pronged conflict, the works of Joseph Stalin and of Mao Tse-tung (Zedong) follow Lenin. Nikita Khrushchev said that the USSR would make ideological concessions when shrimps learn to whistle. In his 1976 report to the 25th Congress of the Communist Party Soviet Union Leonid Brezhnev declared:

Détente and peaceful coexistence are concerned with interstate relations. This means primarily that ... conflicts between countries should not be decided by ... war ... or the threat of force. Détente does not in the slightest way abolish, and cannot abolish the laws of the class struggle.[3]

Leninism has not lost its vitality in the communist world. Much has been written about the changes of position by the French, Italian, and Spanish communist parties — so-called Eurocommunism. In lack of democracy within the parties, they follow Lenin. Whether their promises to the voters to repudiate dictatorship at home and Leninism abroad are tactics to gain governmen-

2. V. I. Lenin, *Collected Works*, v. 23, Lawrence & Wishart, London, 1960, p. 95.

3. L. I. Brezhnev, speech February 24, 1976, published in *Isvestiya*, Mocow, February 25, 1976.

tal control by election and then to be cast aside remains to be seen, but certainly such promises are good Leninism. Consistently with his tenet that the end justifies the means, Lenin's 1917 program published to the Russian people a few months before the Bolsheviks seized power was a model of libertarian democracy. After the seizure, the Party under Lenin made his prepower program a mockery.

In basing the Chinese communist revolution on the peasant Mao said that he was following Lenin but adapting to conditions in China as Lenin would have done. Both Lenin's writings and his deeds confirm Mao. At home Mao and his successors have imposed communist absolutism in emulation of Lenin. Abroad, despite the split with and fear of the USSR, China subverts just as Lenin preached. The gist of China's ideological complaint has been that the Soviets have not pushed Leninism abroad with sufficient zeal.

The extent of deviations from Leninism abroad by some communist-ruled nations may be argued as a matter of scholarly interest, but such a debate would divert attention from the salient points: Lenin preached an unremitting hostility to all capitalist nations and the duty to change their governments to communist by force. The United States is the leading capitalist nation. No Soviet or Chinese communist leader ever has forsworn Leninism, and it is still the guiding ideology of the rulers of both countries.

Lenin planned the transformation of the USSR from its backward state in his day to the industrial and military giant it has become. Despite such material progress at home, Lenin's heirs still hold fast to his ideology and to his tools for advancing it abroad.

Lenin's heirs are not a threat to us because they are socialists. If the communist rulers attempted conversion of the world to socialism only by example and exhortation, Lenin's heirs would not menace us. Nor are socialists as such our enemies. To be sure, socialists who proclaim "no enemies on the left" are dupes or fellow travellers, but some of the staunchest fighters against communist despotism and some of our best European friends have been and are socialists and social democrats. If most of the world's countries adopted socialism but did not try to impose it on other nations by subversion or war, their socialism would not threaten us. Nor do Lenin's heirs endanger us because they reject religion and ethics and brutally oppress at home; there are despicable regimes that are not Leninist. If Albania were the only communist-ruled state, Leninism would not imperil the United States. Lenin's heirs jeopardize our paramount objective because of their implacable hostility to us, because of the double prongs of subversion and war, and because the USSR is one of the strongest nations on earth and China is potentially one of the strongest. With the creed of Leninism superimposed on the nature of men and nations, with the rule by communist masters over more than one-third of humankind, and with the advent of nuclear weapons, the danger to our survival as a free people is serious.

Because of a belief in the west that the communist rulers will mellow, American and European estimates of Leninism have wavered. From the 1920s through détente, the expectation of mellowing has flourished and been disappointed but always has revived.

The expectation has rested on a strange mixture of idealism and cynicism. Some idealists posit that the wickedness inherent in Leninism will give way to a rebirth of goodness, and the brethren will return to the fold. Others — not all of them idealists — assume a misunderstanding, which can be dissipated by patience, persuasion, and cultural exchanges. Let us then build bridges of understanding and take risks for peace. For a good communist this is laughable. He rejects God, despises bourgeois philosophy, and believes in violence. Moreover, he thinks that his way is the path to an eventual materialist paradise on earth.

Seemingly the cynics are more realistic. Every revolution has its Thermidor, they reason; all fires burn out at last. In time men forsake their lofty aspirations and return to the worship of the golden calf. As experience has proved, capitalism produces a cornucopia of material benefits which communism has not equalled; so the communist leaders will change their economic system and abandon their assault on governments in capitalist countries.

Both the idealist and cynical hopes would have a chance to come true if the people of the communist-ruled countries were their own masters. The leaders, however, live in comfort. They wield great power, which they hug to themselves like a beloved; for men prize power even more than gold. The struggle for world domination must go on because by abandoning it the communist rulers would remove the rationale for their dictatorship. Without the cover of Leninism with its ideology of righting all wrongs by a protracted violent conflict with the bourgeois world, the communist emperors would lose their new clothes and stand naked before the world as merely a new breed of tyrants.

Saul was converted and became the apostle Paul after his vision of the Lord Jesus on the road to Damascus where Saul was going to persecute the believers. Mellowing is therefore possible, but prudence dictates that it be given no weight in our estimate of the situation. Leninism enjoins the zigzag to confuse the bourgeois world and retreat in order to resume the advance. We have no way to distinguish between temporary thaws and abandonment of long-range hostility. Mellowing would become credible only after it had been manifested by deeds over a long period of years.

On whether the USSR or the United States started the cold war after World War II, much revisionist history has been written. The hostility between the communist-ruled states and the capitalist countries has not been one-sided. As soon as Lenin seized power in Russia, he started the cold war by subverting all over the world. After the armistice in World War I, the British and French armed intervention against the Bolsheviks in the Russian civil war was hardly friendly. Thereafter, however, England and practically all European nations recognized the communist government in Russia and made treaties with it for trade and friendly relations. Following the ups and downs of diplomatic intercourse between the two sides neglects the deep hostility of the communist-ruled states to all capitalist and even democratic socialist governments. Not only would the communist rulers lose the rationale of their dictatorships by abandoning the struggle; overthrow of capitalist governments is a fundamental tenet of Leninist ideology, which to communists is a religion. The conflict is one that we cannot wish away. It is forced upon us as part of our situation, no matter how much we would prefer that it did not exist.

Someday shrimps may learn to whistle; meanwhile the first

prong of the conflict deserves our scrutiny. The noxious odor of subversion perhaps can be explained by our habit of coupling the word with "communist," but subversion antedates communism by millennia. As the first Book of Kings relates, when King Rehoboam of Israel made heavy his yoke on the people, the northern ten tribes revolted and split Israel into the southern Kingdom of Judah and the northern Kingdom of Israel. The second Book of Kings begins: "Then Moab rebelled against Israel after the death of Ahab."

Although Lenin and his heirs have not disdained influencing subversions to sway governments, their heavy emphasis has been on decisive subversions to overthrow governments. Besides, decisive subversion is the kind that matters in the protracted struggle. Accordingly, the definitions and narrative in this and the next chapter are confined to decisive subversion.

Strictly speaking, an unsuccessful overthrow is not decisive, but this becomes apparent only after the failure. Subversion therefore includes attempted as well as consummated overthrows.

Internal subversion is not one of the statesman's tools; it is employed by dissidents within a country to overthrow their government in all or part of its territory. The American Revolution was an internal subversion of the American Colonies against England. The 1776-1777 aid given to the American rebels against England by France and Spain before each went to war against England was external subversion, an ancient tool of statecraft. The statesman wields it for his government through means other than war by cooperating with internal dissidents in another country in their attempt to topple their government.

The external subverter usually has had purposes of its own. England's reasons for giving arms and money to the revolting American colonies of Spain (1818-1823) were to weaken Bourbon Spain as an expected ally of Bourbon France and to protect England's lucrative South American trade. From the experience of 1793-1815 and of preceding centuries England expected that it would again be at war with France. But whatever the motives of the external subverter have been, the focus of subversion always has been internal. A government cannot overthrow the government of another nation by subversion; only the internal dissidents can.

The internal dissidents have varied from an aspirant to the throne to a large number of the people dissatisfied with their governors. Sometimes both types have combined, as in Absalom's revolt against his father King David; for, as the Bible relates, "the people increased continually with Absalom."

Although occasionally rulers have yielded to the threat of force without its employment, usually the final step in subversion has been the blow by force. When delivered at the top by killing, imprisoning, or exiling the ruler or rulers, the event is called a coup, a coup d'état, or a palace revolution.

By an inside coup, a technique now common in Africa, a legitimate ruler subverts his own government by seizing absolute power. Louis Napoleon was elected president of the French republic and as such destroyed it. After World War II, the communist parties of Bulgaria, Yugoslavia, Rumania, Poland, and Czechoslovakia grasped absolute power by inside coups.

A revolution usually has required a broader application of force than a coup. Either type of overthrow may be followed by a civil war. Both kinds reverse the positions of the governmental Ins and Outs by force or the threat of force, but the wide sociological effects of a revolution are sometimes said to differentiate it from a coup.

This distinction is not borne out by experience. The 1922 coup of Mustapha Kemal that deposed the Turkish Sultan completely altered Turkish society. A coup brought down the last Tsar in March 1917 and substituted a provisional government which allowed freedom of speech and assembly. While a civil war followed the November 1917 Bolshevik "Revolution," this almost bloodless seizure of power was a classic coup. Nonetheless the overthrow abolished the freedoms of the provisional government, restored absolutism, took Russia out of World War I, and transformed the country.

Not every internal subversion has had external help, but the expectation of such help and its giving have strongly stimulated revolution and also have been factors in coups. William of Orange overthrew James II of England in 1688; William's expedition was outfitted in and sailed from Holland. Help from France and Spain kept the American Revolution alive in 1776-1777, and the Americans had counted on the aid. Scholars disagree on whether the 1789 French Revolution and the final overthrow of Louis XVI in 1792 were assisted by English gold, but German money certainly fueled the 1917 Bolshevik Russian Revolution, which in reality was a coup. The Soviet Union assisted Mao's 1949 overthrow of Chiang Kai-shek (Jiang Jieshi). Thus, of the five greatest revolutions from 1688 to our own times, external subversion was a potent factor in four.

Subversion operates through several blades. Generally the cooperation of the foreign subverting government has been by the chief blade of external subversion — the furnishing of money, arms, supplies, or other aid to the internal Outs to help them to become the Ins. The furnishing has been either in the preparatory phase or in the final blow by force. Before Lenin, however, preparatory external subversion did not begin long before the final blow. By a bloodless revolution the pro-French Dutch Patriot Party in power in The Netherlands was overthrown to restore the House of Orange to power and to its English alignment in 1787. But it was not until 1786-1787 that Sir James Harris, the English ambassador at The Hague, financed protest meetings and bought propaganda in Dutch newspapers against the Patriot rule.

Few coups or revolts have been spontaneous; practically all have been plotted and prepared. Before the final blow, the dissidents usually have tried to weaken the government by the preparatory blades of propaganda, agitation, offensive terror, bribery, or some of them.

Before Catherine the Great deposed her husband Tsar Peter III in 1762, she propagandized in the palace guard because it was the decisive group. As inventions have multiplied the mass dissemination of words, the efficacy of propaganda has increased, but words cannot strike the blow by force.

Offensive terror kills persons or damages property to cow the rulers or the people with intent to loosen the grip of the government in order to topple it later. In some cases assassination has been offensive terror; in others the killing of the ruler has been part of the blow by force. In the last quarter of the nineteenth century Russian revolutionists extensively employed assassination as offensive terror. Lenin condemned the practice but was at pains to stress that his disapproval was grounded not on the immorality of offensive terror, but on its ineffectiveness. Experience after World War II might have changed his mind. Offensive terror played a role in persuading Britain to surrender its Palestinian mandate and its Cyprus protectorate and also played a part in the French withdrawal from Algeria.

Defensive terror is not a blade of subversion; it is a government's internal implement which kills, exiles, or imprisons, to suppress present dissidents and to intimidate potential ones. Lenin praised the "regenerative" terror of the French revolutionary government and practiced defensive terror extensively. His heirs have followed his lead.

The writings of Lenin about propaganda were tireless and tiresome, and in *Mein Kampf* (Chapter 6) Adolf Hitler gave the Marxists credit for understanding propaganda's true art. But not even in falsity was either man inventive; the techniques of propaganda are as old as Rome. Our Declaration of Independence, while noble, is nonetheless one of the ablest propaganda documents ever written. In a manual for subversive agents propaganda and each other blade would deserve full treatment, but in following the development of the whole tool, the art of using each blade needs small attention.

The subversive game has two principal players, the internal dissidents and their target government. The latter, however, is not passive; it strikes back. The supporting players are foreign governments helping either side; they can aid the dissidents or the government. But unless the assisting players resort to war, they cannot bring down the target government; this must be accomplished internally.

When Lenin began to practice subversion, predecessors all over the world had developed all the blades of the tool and all the techniques of the final blow. These Lenin accepted, but, as described in the next chapter, he adapted the whole tool to fit his purpose of protracted global overthrow. Despite the complications of the several blades and of any operation, whether in war or subversion, the historical functioning of the whole tool has been comparatively simple.

Traditional subversion — subversion before Lenin and subversion after Lenin that does not apply his adaptation — has created the noxious smell which subversion emits. The tool, however, is not the only source of the stench. With rare exceptions, international politics has been an amoral mixture of brigandage and a confidence game.

The story of traditional external subversion was foreshadowed on the eve of the Peloponnesian War during the discussion at Sparta, where the Corinthian representative said: "There are other ways open to us for carrying on the war. We can foster revolts among the allies [of Athens] . . ."[4] And so the city states against Athens did both during the war and in the interlude of cold war after the Athens-Sparta peace treaty and before the hot war resumed.

The most significant historical pattern has been the recurrence of war. When war has not been in progress, it has been expected to come. Hence, statesmen have been ever busy in trying to change the alignment of foreign governments or to weaken them in a war being waged or anticipated. With this purpose, external subverters have cooperated with internal dissidents to overthrow their government. For the subversion to be useful to the external subverter, it has not been always necessary for overthrow to be consummated. Sometimes an attempt has been a sufficient diversion to accomplish the subverter's purpose. Valentina in north Italy was the scene of fighting between France and Spain in 1626 when Catholic Spain supported financially a revolt in France by Protestant Huguenots. Though abortive, the rebellion induced Cardinal Armand de Richelieu for Louis XIII of France to come to terms with Spain about Valentina.

The key characteristic of traditional external subversion has been its use as an auxiliary to a war in progress or anticipated. Elizabeth I of England thought that Philip II of Spain would attack her sooner or later, as he did in 1588. To keep him busy elsewhere, she gave money and arms to the Dutch who were revolting against Spain's rule over them. French aid to the American Revo-

4. Thucydides, *History of the Peloponnesian War*, Book 1, Ch. 9.

lution was to weaken England in a future war with France. During the Russo-Japanese War, Japan helped to finance the 1905 Russian revolt. In the early years of the twentieth century the Austro-Hungarian emperor supplied insurrectionists against Russia in anticipation of World War I. During it, the German kaiser gave money to the Bolsheviks.

Traditional external subverters were not willing to waste efforts in areas which they thought would not affect the war being waged or anticipated. Before Lenin, there was no global subversion.

Intent on the war in progress or to come, the external subverter has not helped any long sustained preparation to make a government ripe for overthrow. In the rivalry between Spain and England before 1588 and between France and England 1689-1789, Ireland could have been a heavy thorn in the English side. But though Spain and France gave occasional sporadic aid to Irish uprisings, neither made a sustained effort in Ireland. Again because subversion has been auxiliary to war, the help of the external subverter has not been confined to dissidents embracing the same ideology as the subverter. The absolute Louis XVI assisted the libertarian Americans in their revolution.

As the external subverter's estimate of its own situation has shifted, it has turned its flow of aid on and off like a spigot. For a time Elizabeth I of England deserted the Dutch rebels in pursuit of a rapprochement with Philip II. This has been typical. With arms supplied by England, Belgian insurgents revolted against their Austrian ruler in 1789 and drove the Austrians out of Belgium. British Prime Minister William Pitt had furnished the arms to divert Austria from a Russo-Austria attack in progress against Turkey. As soon as Austria agreed to quit the war, Pitt abandoned the Belgians and joined Prussia and Holland, which also had furnished arms to the Belgians, in guaranteeing renewed Austrian rule over Belgium.

In turning off the faucet the external subverter has been callous about the fate of the internal dissidents. In the years of diplomatic preparation for his 1672 war against Holland Louis XIV of France sought a neutrality treaty with Leopold I, Holy Roman (Austrian) Emperor and King of Hungary, but Leopold did not sign. In 1668-1670 Louis promised recalcitrant Hungarian nobles help for an uprising against Leopold, which frightened the emperor about his internal situation. Then to conciliate Leopold, Louis broke off his understanding with the Hungarian nobles and applauded the decapitations that followed. Late in 1671 the emperor signed the treaty which he then broke by going to war against Louis in 1672.

If the recipients of the subversive aid have been less cynical, they have been equally inconstant and opportunist. This has been the rule, as was true in our own history of ingratitude to France during and after the War of the American Revolution. Without French subversive aid in 1776-1777, the infant United States would have prematurely perished. Without the French navy and troops from 1778, we would have lost the Revolutionary War. By making a separate peace with England behind the back of France and in breach of our French alliance treaty, we began to show our gratitude. When France and England went to war in 1793, we declared our neutrality and again broke our alliance treaty. We completed our show of gratitude by Jay's Treaty with England, which favored it at the expense of France in violation of our treaties with France.

Although after the Outs have attained governmental power they have turned their backs on the external subverting nation which helped them become the Ins, perhaps ingratitude is an unfair word. The dissidents have been aware that, except in rare cases, the external subverter has supported them only in its own interest. The union between the parties has been a marriage of convenience in which divorce was to be expected.

Lenin entertained no doubt that his mission was to design a plan for communist conquest of the world. Without this steadfast purpose, a communist would become a mere chatterbox, the kind of person for whom Lenin held only contempt. The real question was by what tool the conquest was to be achieved.

Traditional subversion seemed ill fitted for Lenin's task; war, the second prong of the conflict, appeared to be the tool of choice. By war the Tsars had steadily expanded their domain. All extensive conquerors had selected war as their instrument; subversion had been only war's auxiliary. Lenin changed that relation to fit his mission. As recounted in the next chapter, he modified traditional subversion and made it the preferred communist tool to conquer the world.

As noted in Chapter 2, Lenin's attitude toward war is a favorable factor for nuclear peace, but prudence dictates that we do not assume that the present or a future Soviet leadership will not be adventurous in war. We should not risk our survival on such a conjecture. The double-pronged conflict still jeopardizes our paramount aim not only by subversion, but also by war.

CHAPTER 8

The Fourth of July Tool

For accomplishing our paramount aim, a few kind words about subversion are appropriate. Propaganda, agitation, terror, and bribery are scarcely attractive words. But propaganda can be truthful, and agitation for a just cause is not unethical. Terror is a two-edged blade which can wound the country or cause that uses it, bribery has played only a bit part in overthrow, and neither terror nor bribery is essential for the successful wielding of the whole tool. Even thus cleansed, traditional external subversion has been dirty, but the tool does not have to be used in the traditional manner. The most reviled among the statesman's tools can, if used to overthrow the Leninist rulers, be an instrument for our survival as a free people and for preserving peace.

In April 1976 a Senate select investigating committee issued a voluminous informative but condemnatory report on American clandestine operations since World War II, including the external subversion of our Central Intelligence Agency (CIA). Not once does the Committee mention our own subversive birth.[1] As the then approaching celebration of our two-hundredth birthday might have reminded the Committee, subversion is as American as the fourth of July.

The American revolutionists believed that their internal sub-

1. Report No. 94-755, 94th Congress, 2nd Session, Senate, Book 1, *Foreign and Military Intelligence* and Book 2, *Intelligence Activities and the Rights of Americans*, April 26, 1976, U. S. Government Printing Office, Washington, 1976. See also Preliminary Report No. 94-465, 94th Congress, 1st Session, Senate, *Alleged Assassination Plots Involving Foreign Leaders*, November 20, 1975, U.S. Government Printing Office, Washington, 1975.

version against their lawful sovereign George III was noble. They thought that the 1776-1777 external subversive help that they sought and received from France and Spain — without which the United States would have died aborning — was foreign aid for freedom. Subversion can be ethical. True, practically all internal subversion requires violence, but violence against tyranny is justified. As our Declaration of Independence proclaims: "When a long train of abuses and usurpations . . . evinces a design to reduce [the people] under absolute Despotism, it is their right, it is their duty, to throw off such Government . . ." The abuses and usurpations against which the Americans rebelled were mild compared to those suffered by the people of the communist-ruled nations.

With its foot in its mouth, our CIA has called American external subversion since 1947 "covert action," a sinister sounding phrase. With apt propaganda sense, the communist-ruled states call their external subversion "aid to wars of liberation." So external subversion can be; at its best it is foreign aid for freedom and a good deed.

Leninist subversion is neither aid for wars of liberation nor foreign aid for freedom because communists have replaced every government they have overthrown with a totalitarian dictatorship. American external subversion can be foreign aid for freedom to the communist-ruled people. Not the ethics of such help, but only its wisdom is open to question.

The wisdom turns on whether our assistance will retard or forward our survival as a free people, a question which basic patterns of subversive history illuminate. Traditional external subversion disregarded those patterns because of its use as an auxiliary to war being waged or anticipated. Although the patterns speak for themselves, it is convenient to examine them through the eyes of V. I. Lenin because he was an assiduous student of history from which it was apparent that the traditional tool needed modification to fit his global protracted plan.

Lenin did not have to worry about finding dissidents almost everywhere. In discussing "the instability of the Gauls," Julius Caesar wrote: "In general, they always want to change the existing regime."[2] Niccolò Machiavelli said that a foreign prince "can easily enter [France] by gaining over some baron . . . for one always finds malcontents and such as desire a change." He added: "The lords that remain make themselves the heads of fresh movements against you."[3] As *The Federalist* (No. 28) noted:

> Our own experience has corroborated the lessons taught by the examples of other nations; . . . Seditions and insurrections are, unhappily, maladies as inseparable from the body politic as tumors and eruptions from the natural body; . . .

With rare exceptions, dissidents have been ever present in all countries and from time to time have overthrown their governments. In *The Federalist* (No. 10) James Madison gave the reason — the many causes of factions which are "sown in the nature of man." And as Lenin pointed out, times of trouble have recurred in all countries, have bred dissatisfaction with the government, and have created revolutionary situations.

Internal subversions can be expected to continue because whatever be the form of government, good and wise rulers will not always be at the helm, and some will grossly abuse their power. In consequence, the governed will seek to redress insufferable grievances by overthrowing their governors. The second reason for expecting continued internal subversions, though not praiseworthy, is equally patent and potent: The Outs covet the power the Ins have. The Outs attain power peaceably if they can; if they cannot, from time to time they try to seize it forcibly. Both reasons underlie the plainest pattern in the history of subversion: A government has been a sometime thing.

Machiavelli said that monarchy degenerates into tyranny, which is overthrown by aristocracy, which deteriorates into oligarchy, which is overthrown by democracy, which lapses into license, and is toppled by monarchy.[4] Although history has not

2. G. J. Caesar, *War Commentaries, The Gallic Wars,* Book 4, Ch. 1.

3. N. Machiavelli, *The Prince,* Ch. 4.

4. Machiavelli, *Discourses on the First Ten Books of Titus Livius,* Book 1, Ch. 2. Cf. Aristotle, *Politics,* Book 3, Ch. 7; Plato, *The Republic,* Book 8.

sustained his circular theory or the economic class progression theory of Marx, both men were correct on the normality of overthrow.

While attempted overthrows have far outnumbered successful ones, this observation distracts attention from the principal pattern. The lawful methods of succession to state power have been royal birthright, election, or appointment pursuant to the laws. One unlawful method has been fraud. Royal birthright often has been circumvented by trick and device so that the legitimate claimant did not become king. Emphasis on fraud, however, obscures the proper stress on subversion, which is the other unlawful method of succession to state power. Subversive overthrow has been as normal a manner of changing rulers as the legitimate ways.

Though the United States was born by revolution and saved from disunion by the victory of the North in the Civil War, our government has never been toppled. The Americans south of the Rio Grande River have been far more typical; they have played a serial whose appropriate title might be "Overthrow." And the countries of Europe, Asia, and Africa have experienced many changes of government by force or its threat.

In the ancient world overturning governments by force was regular. Of 26 Roman emperors from Augustus to Maximinus, 16 were assassinated. Medieval history was no different; for the thousand years before 1500 succession by overthrow was ordinary practice. The score in the eastern Roman Empire (364-1453) was 41 out of 118 emperors deposed. In England, out of 17 successive rulers (1087-1452), nine seized power by force, and the period that followed saw one ruler after another fall by violence until Henry VII toppled Richard III in 1485.

Modern history has conformed. A few samples illustrate the whole record. In Turkey (1500-1911), 14 out of 29 Sultans were overthrown by force. Even excluding the period of anarchy in Russia (1610-1613), there were 14 overthrows from 1505 through 1801. France settled down after a series of civil religious wars (1562-1629), but the French government was overturned in 1792, 1794, 1799, 1815, 1830, 1848, 1851-1852, and 1870. Revolution mothered unified Italy (1860-1861).

The fallacy of supposing that legitimate methods have been the only customary way of succession to state power becomes apparent from a look at the present world. Save for Australia, Canada, New Zealand, Japan, India, Israel, South Africa, the United States, and most of western Europe, almost all present governments owe their existence to a subversive overthrow of a preceding government, and in most cases the overthrow has been recent. Moreover, there are few governments whose title deeds do not rest on an overthrow; our own rest on an unlawful overthrow that was nonetheless right.

A planner of a coup or a revolution can study the world history of internal subversion with pleasurable anticipation. Governments have not been forever; they have been structures vulnerable to overthrow. The history of internal subversion teaches that almost everywhere, sooner or later, attempted coups or revolts are to be expected, and many will succeed.

The other basic historical subversive pattern is: Time, place, and outcome of attempted overthrows have been uncertain and unpredictable. A few examples are typical of the historical tenor. When Julius Caesar revolted, the Roman senators with inside knowledge staked their lives and fortunes on Gnaeus Pompey. In 1760 Benjamin Franklin said that a revolt of the Colonies was improbable; its success impossible. Although after the event many volumes have been written about the "inevitable" French Revolution, neither Franklin nor Frederick the Great had anticipated it, and its outbreak surprised the contemporary chiefs of state, among them William Pitt and Catherine the Great. Nor was the place where revolution would occur foreseen; before the event and with reason, observers thought that England was less stable than France. The outcome of the French Revolution was decided by the accident that Louis XVI was a weak monarch with fatuous advisers. A resolute ruler could have nipped the 1789 rising in the bud, and it was the vacillation of Louis until 1792 that finally cost him his crown and head. Had a Henry IV of France or a Pitt been in command, the king would have retained his throne.

In this age of computers, foretelling the where, when, and outcome of attempted overthrow has been no better. When

Nikita Khrushchev was arrested and deposed in the USSR, the United States government and western experts were surprised.

Among the reasons for unpredictability of place, time, and success of attempted overthrow is the variety of the causes. Marxians ascribe revolts almost exclusively to economics, but history does not uphold their claim. In 1775 the Americans were as well off economically as any people on earth, and the burden of taxation in the Colonies was lighter than in the mother country. The Americans rebelled for a freedom of which there was little in their world. The years preceding the French Revolution were among the most prosperous France had ever enjoyed. From 1691 to 1778 when the Irish did not revolt, their economic lot was miserable. It greatly improved from 1778 to 1796 and 1798 when the Irish did rebel. Before the 1821 Greek revolution against the Sultan, the Greeks were prosperous, and those with high standards of living were among the most active revolutionists. People do revolt for political liberty.

Times of trouble foster subversion, but as Lenin pointed out, a time of trouble generating a revolutionary situation does not always bring rebellion. Nevertheless, he generalized his own personal experience by thinking of war as the accelerator of revolution. So it was for Lenin; World War I presented him with a revolutionary situation in Russia. Later Mao Tse-tung (Zedong) took advantage of the chaos which had scarred China since 1911, further promoted by the wake of the long Sino-Japanese wars (1931-1945). But both the American and French Revolutions broke out in time of peace with no external crisis. The 1848 wave of revolts in Europe occurred during peace and 33 years after the end of the Napoleonic Wars.

Who can foresee when an itch for power will be scratched by a coup? Although an aged monarch or a child sovereign frequently has afforded temptation and opportunity, it is impossible to generalize. Louis XIV and Louis XV were boy rulers; neither was deposed. Louis XVI lost his head when he was a mature king.

In overthrow, as in life, luck is an unpredictable variable. Frequently when and where overthrows will be attempted have been strongly affected by the anticipation of foreign help; and often the flow of such aid to the Ins or the Outs, both in the

preparatory stage and in the final blow by force, has determined outcome. Both the promise and the delivery, however,
turn on the subjective factor of who is at the helm of the government furnishing the assistance. There are numerous other
variables, the chief of which is the respective ability of the leaders on the government and dissident sides, a matter of chance.
The many reasons for uncertainty of place, time, and outcome
reduce themselves to the only inevitable — the human variables.

Lenin could have based his expectance of revolutions everywhere sooner or later on Marxism, but uncertainty of time and
place flies in the face of Marxist scientific historical determinism.
As Lenin admitted, Karl Marx and Friedrich Engels believed
that the proletarian revolution would first occur in the advanced
capitalist countries, particularly France and Germany, and not
in backward Russia. Lenin accepted unpredictability of place,
time, and outcome. In 1918 he ridiculed N. I. Bukharin, a faithful
Marxist, for predicting when the German revolution would begin.
Lenin called such a forecast "a blind gamble" and characterized
all such attempts to foretell as "absurd efforts to ascertain what
cannot be ascertained."[5]

Lenin's teaching not only emphasizes uncertainty, but also
negates economics as the exclusive cause of overthrows. Although
Lenin's advice to his heirs on how their subversive work was to
be carried on is scattered through his works, his clearest di-
rections are in *"Left-Wing" Communism, An Infantile Disorder*
(1920). Wherever communists were granted freedom, as had been
true in Russia under the provisional government and as was true
in England, they were to use their liberty to undermine the government, including doing so through participation in parliaments.
Where they did not have liberty, they were to carry on illegal
work underground. Lenin urged taking advantage of every existing discontent in each country, whether economic or not. The
comrades were to agitate about any cause of tension, such as
colonialism and the Irish question in Great Britain. These

5. J. Bunyan and H. H. Fisher, *The Bolshevik Revolution, Documents and Materials 1917-1918,* Stanford University Press, Stanford,
1934, p. 501; V. I. Lenin, *Selected Works,* v. 7, International Publishers, New York, 1943, p. 353.

aspects of communist subversion have been discussed frequently. What has been neglected about *Left-Wing Communism* is how it stresses the uncertainty of time and place of revolt as the reason for protracted perseverance in subversion everywhere. Lenin said that the Dreyfus case in France "was enough to serve as the 'unexpected' and 'petty' cause that brought the people to the verge of civil war!" About England, he wrote: "We cannot say, and no one is in a position to say beforehand, how soon the real proletarian revolution will flare up there, and *what* will most of all serve as the *cause* to rouse it, to kindle it . . ." Hence, he urged his followers "to carry on our preparatory work," and in doing so to "stir up . . . all . . . spheres."[6] Probably it was from the history of subversion that Lenin derived unpredictability of time, place, and outcome; certainly he accepted it.

Lenin started his subversion all over the world as soon as he attained power in Russia. In the spring of 1920 Lenin sent G. Voitinsky and Yang Ming-chai to China to organize the communist movement there. Ho Chi Minh was schooled in Moscow in the early 1920s. Such patience and long-range efforts were rewarded many years later when times of trouble came in China and Vietnam.

Lenin's organizational method was simple. His prime agency was his cherished nucleus, an internal communist party. In 1920 he boasted that he had planted nuclei "in all countries."[7] While he exaggerated, the global coverage he sought was well advanced by the time he died. The nucleus in each country was to be nourished from the external communist-ruled base.

In the method of organizing the external nourishing Lenin erred. Marx had been one of the founders of the International Working Men's Association (London, 1864); it was short-lived. Lenin had castigated the Second International as a renegade to the cause. To replace it, he established the Third International (Comintern) at Moscow in March 1919, liberally financed throughout its existence by the USSR. The Comintern's purposes were to disseminate communist propaganda, to bolster communist parties in all countries, and "to accelerate the development of

6. Lenin, *Selected Works*, v. 10, 1943, pp. 140-143.
7. Ibid., v. 8, 1943, p. 282.

events toward world revolution." At its high point the Comintern had 65 sections in various countries and their colonies. It promoted steady communist propaganda, agitation, and revolts. In 1943 when Joseph Stalin badly needed help from the United States and Britain, he ostentatiously dissolved the Comintern. In 1947 he formed the Cominform as a partial replacement, but it too was dissolved in 1956.

The USSR always firmly controlled the Comintern as its creature. The organizational mistake in Leninist subversion was Moscow's attempt through the Comintern to supervise all communist parties closely. As schools of war teach, an attempt to command in detail from a distance leads to failure. This becomes even more evident when the area is the globe. Local conditions in each country cannot be properly appreciated at the center. Furthermore, control by the USSR gave each national communist party a foreign tinge. The break-up of the communist monolith — which was never really monolithic — has helped communist subversion by stressing the nationalism of each Party.

Lenin incorporated in his subversive tool all the blades and techniques of his predecessors but simply and profoundly modified the whole tool by what may be properly called the Lenin Adaptation. To make the government ripe for overthrow, the internal dissidents were to carry on their preparatory work continuously, and if the blow by force failed, to try, try again.

Trying again was not original. As had been true in Italy, some noncommunist revolutions had succeeded after repeated failures. Generally, however, internal preparation before Lenin had been on and off, and sustained protracted external help had been notable by its absence. Traditional external subversion has been opportunist and spigot; externally the Lenin Adaptation has been usually protracted, sustained, and continuous. The communist-ruled subversive base has given encouragement and financial assistance in the preparatory stage plus arms and supplies when required. Traditional external subversion was always geographically spotty; the Lenin Adaptation is global.

By covering the globe and being willing to wait the Lenin Adaptation capitalizes on the normality of times of trouble and attempted overthrow almost everywhere sooner or later, and the nucleus is ready and waiting to take advantage of opportunity. The supporting base encourages and helps. The global coverage allows for uncertainty of place; the protracted struggle for uncertainty of time. Communist discipline compensates for temporary failure; the loyal comrades close their ranks and try again. Lenin founded a global insurance company of subversion and revolution.

The company advertises its wares, as Marx and Engels did in *The Communist Manifesto* (1848). This is the other difference of the Lenin Adaptation from traditional external subversion, which usually tried to be covert, but practically always failed. A government would be singularly dull if it did not know the source of arms delivery to dissidents or of large injections of money in the preparatory phase. As the Senate Committee noted, CIA covert action has been so generally known as to be covert only in name. In contrast, Lenin shouted from the housetops his intentions to subvert everywhere. Nikita Khrushchev boisterously conformed, as did Mao, and as has Fidel Castro. Even during détente Leonid Brezhnev said that the struggle must continue. While from time to time Joseph Stalin discreetly lowered his voice in pronouncements for consumption in the west, his utterances to be heard abroad managed to tell communists all over the world that the company was still doing business at the old stand in the Leninist way.

This was essential. Lenin's primary reason for announcing openly that the USSR would aid revolution everywhere was to encourage his adherents abroad. There have been revolutions without external help; for example, the English overthrow of Charles I. But the expectation of such aid and its giving have nurtured most internal subversions. And of course overt announcement does not preclude attempted concealment of delivery of money or arms. Communist seizures have been mostly tactically clumsy. Leninist subversive strength has lain in its long-range plan, in patience and persistence in pursuing it, and in the plan's regard for the basic patterns of the tool grounded on the nature of nations.

The Lenin Adaptation has had many failures. During the worldwide depression of the 1930s, for example, the communists tried hard to capture governments, but nowhere did they succeed. Nonetheless, so far the Lenin Adaptation has been a success. Russia was captured after long preparatory work, and the final blow by force was struck during a time of trouble. Because of World War I, Germany supplied the money that would have been given by a communist-ruled base if one had existed. Although Stalin tactically blundered in trying to direct the Chinese communists from a distance, he did help, and with Soviet connivance and protection Mao's forces that overcame Chiang Kai-shek (Jiang Jieshi) were equipped in Manchuria with Japanese arms and munitions, including 2,700 pieces of field artillery and 138,000 machine guns. Internally Mao applied the Lenin Adaptation, long preparation and then the blow by force during a time of trouble. In Vietnam communist internal and external subversion began in the 1920s. By supplying arms the USSR and China aided the final blow by force that won North Vietnam for the communists. Probably it was principally the North Vietnamese army that captured South Vietnam, but the Viet Cong plus Soviet and Chinese arms certainly contributed.

Of the European countries governed by communist parties, Yugoslavia and Czechoslovakia belong to the Lenin Adaptation, but East Germany, Rumania, Hungary, Bulgaria, and Poland were taken under the aegis of the occupying Red Army; the nuclei merely assisted. Albania was never occupied by the Red Army, but before World War II the Albanian nucleus was insignificant.

Both the native nucleus and Koreans in exile trained by the Soviets helped capture North Korea, but under the shield of the Red Army. Cuba and Mozambique were Lenin Adaptation captures; Angola is arguable. As these lines are written, the captures of Ethiopia and South Yemen are too recent for a certain analysis, and Nicaragua still is in flux. The conquest of Afghanistan started by subversion; the USSR finished the job by war.

In 1913 not only was there no communist government on earth, there was not even one socialist government. Besides the captures, the communists are knocking on many governmental doors and have strong nuclei in many countries. It would be misplaced optimism to deny the strength of the red tide. Despite many blunders, Lenin and his heirs have performed well for their side.

Nevertheless, whether the Lenin Adaptation menaces our survival as a free people is a question that cannot be answered with assurance. While vigilance is sensible, on a fair appraisal overthrow of our government by American communists and fellow travelers never has been a serious danger. It does not follow that the Lenin Adaptation does not jeopardize our chief aim; Lenin's heirs may win in the rest of the world by attrition and confront us with an overwhelming aggregation of communist power. If three-quarters of the nations of the earth become communist-ruled, although we might still survive as a free people, there might be enough faint hearts among us to bring about our surrender.

But, as the Sino-Soviet split shows, Moscow will have great difficulty in holding together a communist bloc. The infidelity to the external subverter by Outs who become rulers so testifies. The historical fragility of alliances argues against durability. In the long contest between the Reformation and Counter Reformation, sovereigns shifted sides despite their religious beliefs. Nationalism proved a stronger motive than religion when Catholic France allied itself with Protestant Sweden in the final phase of the Thirty Years' War (1618-1648). With the possible exceptions of the Bulgarians, the people of the Soviet European satellites tolerate communist rule only because the Soviet Army is ready to crush any uprising. The farther a communist-ruled country is from the USSR, the harder it will be for the USSR to control. Still, the bloc might be cemented long enough to be a serious peril to us. In this case patterns clash, and nobody can be sure.

Ever since 1947 we have acted on the assumption that in the interest of our own survival we must hold the line against communist expansion. If we think that we can safely disregard Leninist subversion, we ought to discard containment. But championing American foreign aid for freedom to communist-ruled people is consistent with believing that containment as we have conducted it is a mistake and that the Lenin Adaptation does not menace us. Giving such aid is not based only on defensive grounds. Nor to favor it does one have to be a hardline anticommunist or believe in a crusade against communism. While foreign aid for freedom is ethical, its wisdom rests on the fact that, if successful, foreign aid for freedom will greatly enchance the likelihood of nuclear peace.

Our external subversion since World War II has not promoted that objective; our subversion has been the wrong kind in the wrong places. It is unfair to heap the blame on the CIA for its bag of dirty tricks, the amorality of its subversion, or its mistakes. We owe a debt of gratitude to the agents who have risked their lives and died in the service of our country. Nor were their supervisors in the agency primarily responsible. With rare exceptions, our presidents have tacitly or expressly approved all the actions of the CIA. And if Congress did not know, it was because Congress did not want to know. Let us then give "CIA external subversion" its proper name — external subversion by the United States.

A spate of books and articles plus the Senate Committee report have made an open secret a public record. We have been quite busy in covert action, which in the CIA-Committee definition includes external subversion. From 1952 to the early 1970s we spent more on covert action than on espionage, and since 1961 the CIA has conducted over a thousand covert action projects. Some of the covert actions have been influencing subversions; some defensive secret subsidy, and some defensive paramilitary aid to friendly governments. But we have also sponsored, aided, or conducted a number of attempted overthrows.

The Senate report only mentions two successful ones — the coups that overthrew N. Mossadegh in Iran (1953) and J. Arbenz in Guatemala (1954). Both were traditional opportunist subversions. In Iran, though the communists were the excuse, the probable motive was oil. In Guatemala the coup was defensive to hold the line against communism, which we thought might win if Arbenz continued in power.

The United States abetted the 1963 defensive opportunist coup that overthrew Ngo Dien Diem in South Vietnam because we believed that his internal actions were becoming detrimental to holding the country against the communists. We helped in the 1973 overthrow of Salvador Allende Gossens, again to hold the line against communism. In the Chilean fluid situation the coup had to be opportunist.

We have made some sporadic efforts in the communist-ruled states, notably in Cuba and in China. A 1957 parachute jump into Albania from American airplanes by several hundred saboteurs — mostly Albanian émigrés — was a tragic fiasco because of betrayal by the British traitor H. A. R. Philby. And we propagandized to the European satellites before the 1956 Hungarian revolt, successful until crushed by the Soviet army.

The CIA has defined covert action as "clandestine activity designed to influence governments, events, organizations, or persons in support of U. S. foreign policy conducted in such a way that the involvement of the U. S. government is not apparent."[8] In the last respect the CIA obviously has failed, and as our actions show, "to influence governments" has included trying to overthrow them. We have conducted our subversions in the traditional manner, and in accordance with our policy of containment we have played the game almost entirely in the noncommunist world. That has kept us too busy to exert a major effort to use external subversion where it can promote nuclear peace, and hence our primary aim. We have made no sustained protracted effort to overthrow communist governments.

The weakness of the Lenin Adaptation is defensive because every communist government is a dictatorship. We should learn from the patterns of history and mount a modified Lenin Adaptation in reverse.

That does not mean following our previous pattern of external subversion or entail dispatching a flock of CIA agents to the communist-ruled nations. The first step is to change the rules of the game that the communists have adopted and we have accepted: All noncommunist governments are fair game, but communist captures are irreversible. This we have tacitly acknowledged by containment and our actions. The president should announce that we have rescinded the old rule.

It would be presumptuous to prescribe the form or forum of the declaration, but it should be public and make the following points:

8. Senate Committee Report 94-755, Book 1, 1976, pp. 131, 141.

(1) We are for peace, and we will not go to war to aid communist dissidents.

(2) The attempt of the communist rulers to impose communist dictatorships on all countries endangers peace.

(3) We do not care what economic system the people of any country adopt as long as it is by the voice of the people.

(4) We do not urge the people of the European satellites to revolt and be crushed by communist tanks, but if nuclei form in the satellites to take advantage of a future opportunity, we will consider financial assistance to the nuclei as foreign aid for freedom.

(5) We do not urge the people of the USSR and China to revolt, but because of our revolutionary birth and the oppression they suffer, we are sympathetic to their overthrowing their self-appointed rulers and will consider giving financial assistance to dissidents for preparatory work plus arms if the occasion becomes propitious.

(6) The same will apply to dissidents in other communist-ruled states.

(7) All revolution must come from within; the United States can merely help.

(8) We realize that there are other oppressive regimes, but they do not threaten our survival. While we would welcome change elsewhere and may exhort it, we will not become an international busybody.

(9) The overthrow of the communist rulers is different; it would help not only the people of the countries ruled by communist dictators, but peace which is imperiled by the communist rulers' actions abroad.

(10) While communist subversion has continued, the communist rulers have maintained state diplomatic relations with the western democracies. We shall do likewise with them.

The communist definition of peaceful coexistence permits the governments of communist-ruled countries to employ unlimited subversion. We are only saying that we reserve the right to play by the same definition against them.

The rules we publicly announce should be the ones we observe: no war; no encouragement to premature revolt in the European satellites; encouragement to revolt in all other communist states. We should not try to manage; the internal dissidents will make mistakes, but we would make more by trying to command from a distance or by sending CIA agents to direct. Probably all we can do in the USSR or China at the outset, and probably all we ever shall be called upon to do, is to provide financial help and encouragement. The overthrow may be by a coup. In each country there are enough arms to be seized, and portions of the army may go over to the revolutionary side. Or the armed forces may stand aside. But it would deny the historical patterns and their lessons to predict the unpredictable human variables.

The desired outcome may come internally without our encouragement, but such encouragement always has helped. Its detriment is in giving the dissidents a foreign tinge, but their governments will assert such a tinge in any event and the plus of the help outweighs the minus of the tinge.

The domestic benefits of a democratic overthrow to the people of a communist-ruled state are apparent. The benefit to the American and Soviet people of such an overthrow in the USSR is equally patent; for the overthrow would greatly enhance the chance to keep the nuclear peace. The people of the Soviet Union have no real interest in whether a communist government rules Chile, Zaire, or the United States. Leninism has created the drive of the rulers to impose communist governments on all nations; Leninism has generated the implacable hostility of the communist rulers to the United States. If that creed ceased to be sacred doctrine in the USSR, in all likelihood Soviet hostility to the United States would evaporate.

An overthrow in one of the communist outposts would not be as valuable for peace as one at the core. But such an overthrow would shatter the illusion of irreversibility and give heart to dissidents in the Soviet Union.

Prosperity is subordinate to our chief aim, but foreign aid for freedom will not be expensive, even though some of the money will be wasted and embezzled. The cost will be a drop in the bucket compared to the money we spend for subsidy.

George F. Kennan, the architect of containment, has asserted that popular revolt against a ruthless experienced modern dictatorship "is simply not a possibility."[9] Perhaps his opinion is why he advocated containing communism in the rest of the world rather than undermining its bases. Even if Kennan is correct about the USSR and China, his assumption does not hold true for a dictatorship that has not been able to tighten its grip, as was the case before Congress abandoned giving arms to the Angolan insurgents during Gerald Ford's administration. As these lines are written, the Angolan situation is still fluid. Under Ford and Henry Kissinger, the CIA was busy with traditional subversion in Africa. Jimmy Carter wisely did not send American troops to oppose the Cubans, but his faith in deploring and diplomacy has been mistaken. He should have sent American foreign aid for freedom after open announcement. He should have said bluntly: The Cubans are foreign intruders in Africa. To any Africans willing to kill the Cuban intruders, the United States will give cannon. And the weapons we supply will match in quality the Soviet weapons.

More fundamentally, Kennan neglects the long history of subversion. If dictatorial tyrannies had been invulnerable to overthrow, no tyrant ever would have been overthrown. While the Soviet and Chinese rulers have been adept at repression, so have been their despotic precursors all over the world. And like their predecessor dictators, neither the Soviet nor the Chinese leaders have been models in the art of suppressing; they too have bungled and may be expected to bungle again. As the 1979 fall of Iran's Shah Mohammad Reza Pahlavi showed, if the latent causes of overthrow are present, overthrow is never impossible.

Latent conditions for an overthrow exist in the USSR. One of them is the long-standing nationalities problem; only a little more than half of the people are Russians, and soon they will be less than half, yet Russians dominate the bureaucracy. A relatively tiny percentage of the people belong to the communist party, whose members receive the plums. There were struggles for the succession at the death of Lenin and of Stalin; Khrushchev was deposed.

The armed forces are a potential dagger. When the dagger

9. G. F. Kennan, *On Dealing with the Communist World,* Harper, New York, 1964, p. 11.

will be plunged is impossible to predict, but to say that it will forever remain in its sheath disregards history. From Rome to our own day a standing army, though necessary for defense against enemies abroad, and though often the shield of the rulers, also frequently has been the agent of their overthrow. As *The Federalist* (No. 41) put it: "A standing force . . . is a dangerous, at the same time that it may be a necessary, provision." True, modern weapons are more deadly than ancient ones, but, as Mao pointed out, men fire them. If some of the men or officers turn their weapons on their rulers, the character of the weapons will not matter.

To compete in the technological age, the rulers have had to educate the people. While the masters have tried to channel education by indoctrination, the educated learn to think, and thought bursts through the levees that seek to hold it within the communist stream. But over and above all these and other conditions is the repression of freedom. "Why are ye fearful, O ye of little faith?" People do revolt for liberty.

The March 1917 Russian revolution and the 1911 Chinese revolution had strains of freedom within them. It was no accident that the Bolshevik 1917 platform promised in detail every conceivable democratic freedom, even including the recall of judges by the people. Although Sun Yat-sen, the father of the 1911 Chinese revolution, envisioned a period of tutelage, he too promised freedom.

Besides liberty, there is the peasant yearning for land. In 1917 Lenin made an alliance with the Left Social Revolutionary Party, the representative of the peasants. He promised land ownership and temporarily allowed it. Then he began taking it away, and Stalin largely finished the taking.

Mao promised the Chinese peasants land, let them have it for a while, and then deprived them of it. In China shared want is imposed on one of the ablest commercial people on earth, who abroad have risen to affluence by their hard work and acumen.

The people of the USSR and China are not fools. They may seem to accept the lies and changes of line to which they have been repeatedly subjected, but they must see through them.

Among the latent causes of overthrow are those sown in the nature of man. As James Madison noted, no system of government ever has been able to insure that able rulers will always be at the helm. Not only are dictators persons; they are served by persons. No tyrant rules alone; he governs through human beings who are subject to the emotions, passions, jealousies, and ambitions to which flesh is heir. In all communist states contenders for rule have clawed each other mercilessly in their struggles for power. A future clawing may give rise to a situation that a leader of the people may exploit.

Contemporary visitors to the USSR have observed that the people, though dissatisfied with the system, are more interested in personal advancement within the system than in its overthrow. Perhaps, but who knows when a leader will arise to fire their hearts? Who could have predicted in late 1916 that Lenin, an obscure expatriate revolutionist, would become the chief of state of Russia a year later?

Contemporary observers frequently have been mistaken. In 1974 Ray Vicker, an experienced reporter who has long been familiar with the Arab countries and who speaks their languages, concluded after one of his many visits to Lebanon that the Lebanese of all classes were entrepreneurs who above all else were devoted to money making, at which they were "particularly adept." While he noted the presence of the Palestinians, any reader of his narrative would infer that the delightful Lebanese oasis in the Arab world that Vicker portrayed would remain green, flourishing, and undisturbed by upheaval.[10] Vicker's 1976 articles in *The Wall Street Journal* graphically depicted quite a different scene.

Lenin's own case is evidence of the fallibility of current reporting about when the fire will break out. When Lenin heard the news of the overthrow of Nicholas II, at first he would not believe it.

Admittedly there is a strong authoritarian tradition in both Russia and China. But in 1789 France had an equally strong authoritarian tradition. The title of the Bourbon king was legitimate; he and his forebears had sat on the French throne for 246 years. Yet Louis XVI lost his throne and his head.

10. R. Vicker, *The Kingdom of Oil*, Scribner's, New York, 1974, Ch. 11.

Foreign aid for freedom is contrary to the theory of détente that the Soviets can be won over by wooing them with trade, pleasant talk, and the like. Under the aura of détente the USSR has become more and more adventurous in accordance with one of Lenin's chief tactics: Press against weakness; retreat before strength.

The Soviets will use for propaganda our public announcement of foreign aid for freedom, but the declaration will seem no great change to them. It is a tenet of communist ideology that bourgeois nations will attempt to overthrow communist rulers, and however much we say the opposite, the Soviet rulers do not believe us. Our playing by their rules will not stop arms limitations treaties if the USSR believes them to be in its interest nor will the Soviets go to war because they are annoyed.

Under foreign aid for freedom we shall send not a single American soldier abroad. Moreover, when we act on the assumption that a communist capture of a government is reversible, we shall be more reluctant to prop up oppressive governments. Far from causing American wars, foreign aid for freedom will tend to prevent them. If we had not thought that Vietnam would be lost once it fell to the communists, we would not have waged our Vietnamese war.

To maintain that foreign aid for freedom will assure our survival would be to claim too much. The effort may fail, and if it succeeds, no one can say when. Other measures for our survival still will be required. But because the benefits of foreign aid for freedom outweigh its detriments, we ought to pursue it persistently and steadily.

No one can prove that the communist masters will be overthrown, and no one can prove that they will not. All that can be said is that the patterns of history suggest a fair chance of success, but the timing is impossible to foretell. To try to write the play as it will happen would be to fall into the trap of denying the historical pattern. The only certainty is that no one can be sure.

Prudence and inaction are not synonymous. External subversion as foreign aid for freedom can be an instrument of peace.

In furtherance of our survival as a free people we will honor our heritage when we wield the fourth of July tool.

* * * * *

In closing it is well to remember the beginning. Few would dispute that our paramount objective is survival as a free people. Our mistake has been in application; we have failed to test decisons of moment by our primary aim.

Because history records a longer and wider experience than any human being can accumulate in a lifetime, historical experience is the best teacher. From history it becomes apparent that the nature of nations and of the people who compose them has not altered appreciably enough to affect in a significant degree the patterns which history has traced.

Although we cannot pierce the veil of the future to predict particular events, we can learn the characteristics, capacities, and limitations of the tools of statecraft from the patterns woven by their operation through the ages. Important to every estimate of the situation is the silent factor of what each tool can and cannot do. It is bootless to choose a policy without knowing which tools are capable of carrying it out and whether we are willing to employ them.

Between increasing the strength of our nuclear sword and SALT, the former is the right choice. The other specific prescriptions for survival — shelter by civil defense and a shield against incoming nuclear missiles — are hard to controvert once one realizes that nuclear war is likely sooner or later. Even if one believes that nuclear war is unlikely, it cannot be validly denied that nuclear war is reasonably possible.

Not rhetoric, but disposition of our forces is important for peace. To maintain it we should bring our troops back home gradually and with fairness to our allies. The other affirmative action for both our survival and peace is wielding the fourth of July tool.

The elimination of error is a necessary step in arriving at conclusions. Hence negative proposals are as important as affirmative ones. No need to reiterate the don'ts, however; for if we build on the suggested foundations and add the characteristics of all the tools, knowing what not to do becomes evident.

None of the suggested actions is unethical; so there has been no need to defend their morality except with regard to foreign aid for freedom. A high ethical standard for the United States government is right, but about the good faith of any government the healthy skepticism of the founding fathers is the attitude dictated by history.

Only the chapter on bringing the boys back home presumes to advise other nations what to do. That exception stems from a proper sense of humility about our own power and wisdom. In the long run, ending the dependence of our allies upon the United States will be good not only for us, but for them.

Though the focus here has been on the United States, the characteristics of the tools have enduring and universal application. Nor is the essence of the intangibles confined to our country or the present. Situations differ, but the doctrine of the situation does not. All democracies will continue to share the same long-range aims. The gauge of prudence and its limitations apply everywhere. Neither time nor place alters how to maintain fortitude on the home front. Détente and containment may fade away, but interposing policies between objectives and situation still will be erroneous in the year 2000 and in every country.

In a strict sense, I do not regard the preceding recommendations as mine. Whenever a historical pattern has conflicted with a tentative theory of my own, I have bowed to the pattern and discarded the theory. The do's and the don'ts stem from objective, situation, and tools save for Chapter 6 where I chose between dangers.

We Americans are fortunate to live in a country that allows its citizens the greatest liberty that has ever existed on this earth. Perhaps a few nations equal us in this respect; none surpasses us. Our rights, however, impose on each of us the correlative duty to help in steering our nation's course. Survival and peace are the business of us all.

Index